B.C. Gippid

1982

A Fierce Personal Pride

Despite Frank's dictatorial ways, J.K. did not hesitate to challenge him. When Knowles suggested a printing department, J.K. resisted because of his experience in another plant: "I want no printing at the start, anyway. I learned better at Dunnell's. It's a seasonal business, unreliable, dependent upon style. We'd need skilled help, well-paid union men—sketch makers, color mixers, engravers." From the start, unionism had no place in Mount Hope's concept of management. Frank relented on the matter of a printing department and told J.K. to do as he wished.

Under Frank's leadership, capital was soon pledged and the old mill property was bought from New England Cotton Yarn Co., of which he was president. Of this deal Frank said with a sudden smile, "We'd have paid less if I hadn't been on both sides of the bargain." Frank became chief stockholder of the firm, and J.K., the least important minority holder. Capital of $125,000 was invested in 1,250 shares at $100 par. Four of Frank's New Bedford friends bought shares: William W. Crapo, a wealthy lawyer who had ac- quired textile interests through his practice; Thomas S. Hathaway and James E. Stanton, Jr., both officers of the Acushnet and Hathaway Mills; and Henry L. Tiffany, founder of the Kilburn Mill and a member of the family of well-known New York City jewelers. Frank Knowles invested $50,000 (for five hundred shares); Crapo and Hathaway $25,000 each; Stanton and Tiffany $10,000 each; and J.K. Milliken, $5,000. The company was incorporated on June 13, 1901, and two days later investors were assessed $100 for each share owned, thereby doubling capital. Uncle Frank became president, and J.K., who was to be chief operating officer, was named treasurer.

J.K. began by besting his uncle in another test of wills. Frank felt that the old plant should be razed and a new one built. J.K. convinced him, however, that the old wooden structure could be retained and expanded as necessary. Within ten days workmen had begun a small brick addition where bleaching and dyeing were to be done and other departments housed, including the grey room, where incoming goods were prepared for finishing.* A new boiler was added to supplement two old ones, and a Corliss engine was installed. An elevated water tank was raised above the plant, and water and steam lines added. Mount Hope Finishing was under way.

It promised to be a stormy voyage. J.K. had found an engineer to plan the work, and Frank had advised him: "If you hire these people you'll probably get about the same service whatever the price, so make the best trade you can." J.K. heeded this advice, and soon afterward, his Uncle Frank asked him for details of the engineering contract. "They agreed to $800," J.K. said, with a trace of pride in his voice. "For God's sake," Frank snapped. "What do you expect to get for *that?*" In this case, as in many others, there was no satisfying Frank.

Milliken was not intimidated; he knew his uncle well. "Everything I proposed, he would argue. I'd go to his house and tell him some plan and get thoroughly sat on. I'd come back cursing him because he wouldn't agree to what I thought right. . . . The next time I saw him he would ask in a perfectly quiet voice what I had done, fully expecting, apparently, that I'd gone ahead exactly as I had planned." J.K. came to the conclusion that his uncle believed "it was best for all of us for him always to take the opposite view on everything and make me prove my point. I don't remember his ever admitting that I was right in anything." Yet the domineering Knowles never actually lost his temper with his nephew and, in his exasperating way, allowed him a certain independence. J.K. remembered his uncle's methods: "When he had said all he wanted and we didn't reach an understanding, he had a way of looking at me that said, 'I didn't believe anyone could be as dumb as you are,' and that ended it. . . . As I look back on it, I realize that for a man so positive and self-sufficient, he yielded his viewpoint in many re-

Grey, in the textile trade, is also rendered *greige*, meaning a color between grey and beige. Origin: French for raw, or untreated. First documented usage was 1926. Oxford English Dictionary.

business came not only from the neighboring towns in the heart of the New England cotton textile industry; J.K. made occasional trips to New York and Boston, where he found that Uncle Frank's reputation opened many doors to him, and he was able to attract customers who were to remain Mount Hope standbys for many years.

The first few years in North Dighton also brought major changes in Milliken's personal life. A son, Robert Dodds, born in 1904, became the first of four children. Helen was born in 1905; J.K., Jr. (who was to be called Pete), in 1907; and Ruth, in 1910. J.K. often said that he refrained from naming his firstborn J.K., Jr., since, "I wasn't sure it would be a success, and I didn't want a failure connected with my name. By the time Pete came along, it was clear that Mount Hope was a success, and so I named him after me."

Mount Hope stockholders were soon rewarded by the industriousness of workers and management. Volume had risen from $175,000 in 1903 to $430,000 in 1907, with profits climbing from $1,300 to $35,000.

In 1907 J.K. made an important physical change at the plant, bringing a spur track of the New York, New Haven and Hartford Railroad to Mount Hope's siding and retiring the faithful Percherons and their drivers.

In the same year J.K. was offered a position as head of a rival finishing firm, an old, well-established plant in the area. Milliken gave serious consideration to the offer, but Uncle Frank advised against the move, warning J.K. that he was likely to discover unexpected difficulties if he stepped into an unfamiliar situation. Frank tempted his nephew to remain as executive head of Mount Hope by increasing capital stock by 250 shares, all to be sold to J.K. at par, but not immediately. As J.K. recalled the transaction: "It was spread out over 25 years like a feedbag ahead of a horse to keep him going. And the more it became worth, the more it would mean to me. . . . I thought it was pretty scrimy, but it was a gift horse and I never thought it good judgment to look a gift horse in the mouth."

Though he never failed to express himself on the company's affairs for the remainder of his life, Frank had now passed the torch to J.K. Milliken, and a singular succession of family managers had begun.

"I must go it alone"

The heritage of the founders of Mount Hope traced back to the Pilgrim settlement of Plymouth, where the first American of the Knowles family arrived in 1637. Richard Knowles, an English seaman, eventually moved to Eastham, in a section later to become known as Orleans. His descendant Thomas Knowles was born here in 1803. Thomas was the son of Thomas and Alice Pepper Knowles and was destined to become the first wealthy member of the clan, the creator of the capital that was to make possible the founding of Mount Hope Finishing Company.

This early Knowles fortune was amassed in the whaling trade in New Bedford, where Thomas Knowles settled as a young man, probably drawn by the prosperity brought to the small port city by the far-ranging fleets of whalers. Thomas was soon in business for himself, trading as Thomas Knowles and Company. He was cross-eyed and, in the words of a descendant, was "exceedingly shrewd and domineering and none too particular about the methods he used to attain his ends."

Thomas was less interested in owning whaling ships than in outfitting the vessels and crews with supplies, and his firm grew rapidly with the expansion of the whaling trade. New Bedford seamen had been whaling for almost a century when, in 1835, the first right whale was taken, and the volume of oil coming into the port increased dramatically. In that year Thomas took in as partner his brother John Knowles, who had been at sea for many years, a man who was equally "independent, arbitrary and dictatorial." The firm became Thomas and John F. Knowles, but, though more prosperous than ever, it was frequently shaken by clashes between the strong-willed brothers.

A year later, in 1836, Thomas took into the firm as clerk his young cousin Joseph Knowles, from the family home in Eastham, a promising teenager who had recently graduated from Phillips-Andover Academy. The new clerk, so Thomas hoped, would side with him in his bitter controversies with the headstrong John Knowles—and was also expected to handle the company payroll and deal with the public, roles for which the abrasive older men were unsuited. Young Joseph was hired at the princely salary of $50 per year until he was nineteen, when the rate would increase to $75 per year—and then advance to $100 before he reached the age of twenty-one. Even these terms were liberal for the time, so Thomas assured his cousin.

These were exciting years in bustling New Bedford, capital of the North American whaling trade. Herman Melville, who visited the town while Joseph Knowles was still a clerk, wrote of it in *Moby Dick*: "The town itself is perhaps the dearest place to live in, in all New England. . . . nowhere in America will you find more patrician-like houses; parks and gardens more opulent, than in New Bedford. When came they? . . . All these brave houses and flowery gardens came from the Atlantic, Pacific and Indian oceans. One and all they were harpooned and dragged up hither from the bottom of the sea."

Joseph Knowles, obviously the stuff of which diplomats are made, not only survived the stormy conflicts between his cousins, but in

Ship Falcon,
 John Wells,
 Minerva 2d.
 Tamerlane.
Bark Charleston Packet,
 Edward,
 Hecla,
 Isabella,
 Robert Morrison,
 Undine,
 Wave.

Thomas Knowles and Company whaling signal. (Courtesy of Old Dartmouth Historical Society, Whaling Museum, New Bedford, Mass.)

1844 he was taken in as a full partner and helped to direct the increasingly prosperous firm during the heyday of New Bedford's whaling trade. The following year, when the trade reached its peak, ten thousand seamen brought into the port more than 430,000 barrels of whale and sperm oil, in addition to three million pounds of whalebone. Some whalers were on the seas for as long as ten years before returning, and voyages of three to five years were not uncommon. The oil they brought home provided light for thousands of American homes, supplied young industries, and lubricated the working parts of numerous household appliances, from cider presses to clocks and watches. The whalebone was used in corset stays, fans and other feminine accoutrements. It was also the whaling ships, touching at the Azores, that brought to New Bedford Portuguese immigrants, the first newcomers to a region settled and dominated by Anglo-Saxons. Wealth came in the train of the whaling trade, but vice flourished on the waterfront in an area known as "Hard Digs," where brothels, bars and gambling dens spawned an epidemic of robberies, murders and violence that was ended by an indignant local mob, which burned the waterfront dives. Almost unnoticed in the tumult of the whaling boom, the first large New Bedford cotton mill, the Wamsutta, opened in 1846, and the textile industry began its steady growth in the region.

By now Joseph Knowles had married Jedidah (Jeddy) Doane of Orleans, and Helen, the first of their children, was born in 1847. Their third child, Joseph Frank Knowles, was born in 1853.

Thomas and John Knowles, the senior partners, had by this period become leading citizens of the town, bank directors and men of influence in business affairs and politics. Thomas, a strong Temperance man, once ran for mayor on the Temperance ticket and was narrowly defeated. With the coming of the Civil War, Thomas invested most of his wealth in government bonds and vigorously supported the war effort. As a leading Abolitionist, he supported the Underground Railroad by which slaves escaped to freedom.

The Knowles firm prospered throughout the war. In the spring of 1865 it suffered its greatest loss when the bark *Edward,* one of its eleven whaling vessels, was burned by the Confederate raider *Shenandoah*—a remarkable ship that went on to burn more than half the U.S. whaling fleet in the north Pacific before its final surrender in England, seven months after Appomattox.

During the war, Thomas Knowles foresaw the doom of the whaling trade—the first oil well had opened at Titusville, Pennsylvania, in 1859—and under his urging, the firm of Thomas Knowles and Company was liquidated in 1872. Thomas and Joseph invested their funds in western mortgages for a time, but John, who did not share their vision of the future, remained in the whaling trade and eventually became a bankrupt, paying his creditors ten cents on the dollar. Thus the brothers had gone their separate ways, one profiting by his foresight and the other, insensitive to changing times, failing in his declining years. It was Joseph the erstwhile clerk who profited most spectacularly by investing in the booming New England textile industry, which was beginning to achieve dominance in the business life of the region. By now the head of a mature family, Joseph put most of his share of the accumulated profits of the whaling firm into cotton mill stock, a timely and fortunate investment.

An even more astute investor was Joseph's son Joseph Frank, who was nearing age twenty when Thomas Knowles and Company left the whaling trade. Frank was to become one of the ablest of the family's men of business, a strong-willed character in a family noted for its bold, colorful men. Though it was not yet obvious, Frank had been preparing for a career in industry for several years. To the traits of his father, he added those of his mother's family connections—Doane and Hatch—clans which had been prominent in the region for generations. His parents sometimes despaired of Frank's habit of wry, sarcastic joking, but he had grown up as a well-educated, ambitious and highly motivated young man. His mother, Jeddy Doane Knowles, had been educated at Wilbraham

Academy and had taught school. Frank had attended Friends Academy in New Bedford and entered M.I.T., but though he was a gifted engineer, he had failed to graduate, a mystery explained by his family succinctly: "He may have made himself positively a nuisance," the theory being that Frank's penchant for argument and badinage may have offended some professor. Frank's father guided him to his first job in the dye house of the Star Mill in Middleboro, Massachusetts, the first step in a career that was to have an enduring effect on his heirs and associates.

The boy had been at work less than a year when his father died. The elder Joseph Knowles, though a strong, virile man, succumbed quickly to pneumonia, for which there was then no effective treatment. The soundness of Joseph's investments in textile mills now became obvious, for he had left an estate of $150,000, a tidy fortune for that day. By family agreement the estate was allowed to remain intact during the life of his widow, Jeddy.

At his mother's insistence, Frank returned to New Bedford, where he found a job in a cotton mill controlled by a well-known local banker, Jonathan Bourne. The autocratic Bourne, who was also the scion of an old whaling family, taught Frank the art and science of bookkeeping so effectively that the youngster was soon working for a competitor, a Mr. Brayton, who was a cotton broker. Frank entered the office of the Union Manufacturing Plant in Fall River, which had been taken over by Brayton. When Brayton told a friend he was in search of an honest bookkeeper and inquired about Frank Knowles, he was told, "You don't want him. He's too much of a man for a bookkeeping job. He can run the mill." Brayton replied, "Then he's just the man I want."

Frank's education was advanced by the stern Brayton, another of the fiercely independent men who led New England industry in that era. Brayton, it was remembered, was so stingy that a workman claiming that he needed a new broom had to first bring in a worn-out handle for inspection.

Young Knowles began work with Brayton about 1880, forming a

friendship that was to last for life, but only two years later, confident that he was ready to embark on his own, Frank returned to New Bedford and became owner and operator of a new mill. After the briefest of apprenticeships in textiles, he founded the highly successful Acushnet Mill. Though Knowles was only twenty-eight years old, Bourne and Brayton were so favorably impressed with his ability that they backed the enterprise with the necessary capital.

In 1886, Frank married Angeline, the daughter of George Bourne, a leading auctioneer and real estate dealer. The couple had three children within a few years. In 1888 Frank founded a second mill, the Hathaway, which was also immediately successful. He remained treasurer and clerk of Acushnet and Hathaway for life. Following the example of his father, Frank poured virtually all of his family's assets into textile mills—the funds of his mother, brother and sisters as well as his own—and invested substantially in the Union, Sagamore, Border City and other mills in the area. Throughout his career, Frank was backed financially by wealthy men of New Bedford who had known him since his infancy and were impressed by his abilities.

Though he was frequently as domineering as the whaling captains of his lineage, Frank was personable and attractive; the unorthodox traits revealed in his youth became pronounced eccentricities only in the latter years of his life. He was a small man of less than five feet six inches who never weighed more than 150 pounds and much less after middle age. He had a high forehead and fine, thin hair that turned gray prematurely. His small hands were mobile and expressive. His tiny mouth, which often curled in a puckish grin, was usually clasped about a cigar. Childhood illness had left Frank subject to frequent headaches, and weak eyes forced him to work in a darkened office and to wear an eyeshade. One of his numerous ailments was diagnosed as hardening of the arteries in his eyes.

Frank never drank liquor. He ate lightly, though always rapidly. He took no regular exercise and was troubled by sleeplessness for most of his life—yet he drove himself relentlessly throughout his business career, and in addition to operating his own mills and helping to direct others, he became father confessor, counselor and investment officer for the entire family.

Since he had married late in life, and loved the company of children and young people, Frank spent much time with his nieces and nephews, especially the children of his older sister, Helen Knowles, whose marriage to Charles D. Milliken had ended in separation. Milliken, who came from Farmington, Maine, was the operator of a dry goods store in New Bedford. In the absence of the father, Frank became, in effect, the foster father of Helen's son Joseph Knowles Milliken, who was known as "J.K." Though they were frequently engaged in a conflict of wills reminiscent of the travails of Thomas Knowles and Company, Frank Knowles and his nephew developed a close and understanding relationship that ended only with Frank's death.

Frank romped and played with Helen's children during their early years, and J.K. retained a lifelong memory of how his uncle shed his dignity when he entered the house, to tumble about on the floor with him. Frank entertained the children by snatching up their ill-tempered cat by the tail, adroitly avoiding bites and scratches, to drop it, snarling and spitting—only to have the animal run expectantly to its tormentor on the next visit, apparently anxious for more fun. The children also remembered Frank's habit of singing loudly while shaving: "Polly Wolly Doodle All the Day," or "Climbing Up Those Golden Stairs." Though they were twenty-two years apart in age, Frank and J.K. began sailing the waters off Rhode Island and southeastern Massachusetts during the years of J.K.'s boyhood and continued for many years in ever-larger boats.

Young J.K. was an avid and gifted student, and was sent to Harvard by his grandmother, who saw to it that he had an adequate allowance. Jeddy Knowles, who depended on her son Frank in every way, probably followed his wishes in sending J.K. to college, but Frank apparently made few further efforts to guide his nephew's course. His only advice, as J.K. recalled it years afterward, was the pointed remark, "Get some knowledge of chemistry. There's no place in my mills for you—you must learn something we don't know." J.K. did not heed this advice, but he did finish Harvard in three years, a rare accomplishment for that day.

Although he completed his Harvard work early, J.K. waited until 1896 to take his degree with his class. He then started work in the Dunnell Finishing plant in New Bedford, where he began learning the textile business from Henry Dunnell, a nephew of the treasurer and major stockholder. Four years later, when the mill was undergoing a reorganization, J.K. was "summarily bounced" when the Dunnells discovered that Frank Knowles was his uncle and concluded that the youngster was an industrial spy.

J.K. spent a few weeks restlessly awaiting another chance for a job before Frank offered him a place in the Hathaway Mill as a bookkeeper, a field entirely new to the ambitious youngster. But though he knew literally nothing of double entry bookkeeping, J.K. applied himself so effectively that Uncle Frank transferred his incumbent bookkeeper to another mill ten days later.

J.K. never forgot his trying days of apprenticeship: "I got off a trial balance at the end of the first month after much difficulty, and then saw that I could get a lot of information off that balance sheet. I posted the bills, prepared the checks for his signature, dunned the people who owed us money, figured the payroll, got it at the bank . . . paid off, and of course kept the cash book and ledger." After overhearing Frank's merciless scolding of other bookkeepers who were tardy with their accounts, J.K. resolved to put the trial balance on the treasurer's desk on the first day of each month, though he had but a few hours to assemble the final figures. Frank accepted this miracle without comment, and it was years later when J.K. learned that his uncle had asked his sister Grace in a tone of grudging admiration, "Does he work nights?"

J.K. soon learned his uncle's methods of money management. Each quarter, as the dividend date neared, J.K. was required to have the checks on his uncle's desk well in advance so that they might be signed at his convenience. Each quarter Frank accepted the balance sheet and returned it to J.K. with inventory figures that would provide a profit of precisely $20,000 for the period, not a penny more or less—just the amount he intended to pay in dividends. Frank once came near a permanent rupture with his veteran accountant F.S. Fuller over his highly unorthodox methods of bookkeeping.

Fuller told Frank one day, "You're the only person I ever saw who managed to get his inventory over on the liability side of the ledger."

"That's the way I want you to present the books."

Fuller refused.

"Yes, you're going to do it."

"I can't. I won't. Get another auditor."

"I can't do that. You know everyone would be too upset."

But though he was unable to persuade Fuller to do his bidding, he obliged J.K. to keep the books as he directed. When a friend asked Frank how he managed to pay dividends in his unique way, the creative treasurer merely laughed. When his cash position permitted, Frank summoned up the necessary profits as if by magic and rewarded his stockholders with an extra dividend. In all of this Frank insisted upon the utmost secrecy. J.K. remembered: "He hated publicity. He went so far one time as to pay a dividend which was distributed not by the mill's checks but by the checks of Mr. Crapo, Mr. Hathaway, and others."

Frank also led an active public life and was for years a leading figure in New Bedford's affairs. He frequently declined offers to run for mayor. He was a major influence in the New Bedford Cotton Manufacturers Association but also supported the Protecting Society, the Free Library of Bristol County, and the Congregational Church. He served as an Alderman for four years.

But his mills were his first love, and it was there that he spent most of his waking hours. J.K. Milliken's training during two years at Hathaway was by no means limited to poring over the mill's books. Frank gave occasional hints of his awareness of his role as the mentor of a future leader of the American textile industry, a role in which he was to leave his stamp upon the Milliken family enterprise for generations.

Frank was given to tossing off epigrams to his nephew, many of which were not to be forgotten: "It's not what a man does that counts," Frank said. "It's what he gets other people to do." This principle was to work wonders in Mount Hope's future. Frank urged J.K. to constant vigilance in business: "There's no such thing as standing still. You're either going ahead or going behind." He repeated one piece of advice in a variety of ways, the gist of which was: "If a man has a winning spark in him you can make a lot out of him—but if he hasn't, the sooner you drop him, the better."

It was not always the voice of the hardened executive that the young man heard from his uncle. Once, near the end of his life, when unexpected business burdens had sapped his strength and will, Frank told J.K., 'I've forgotten how to play. You must never get into that position."

Frank's creative approach to the problems of the textile trade provided models for the future Mount Hope Finishing Company. He was among the first New England manufacturers to grasp the potential of operating his own finishing plant and employing a commission house to sell the goods he produced in such quantities. To reduce his dependence upon printers who bought his output, he devised the means of styling, finishing and distributing his own products—a miniature application of the methods of the vertical firms of a later era. Soon, however, he replaced the commission house with his own sales organization which he based in New York under direction of a single trusted employee. Frank maintained daily contact with the New York office, a pattern that would become familiar in the Mount Hope operation.

One of Frank's singular habits was to be taken up in turn by his nephew and by J.K.'s son and grandson in turn. Frank kept a small notebook in which he recorded almost everything of importance in his daily rounds to provide a log for future reference. He also made engineering computations there on the performance and capacity of machinery; he figured his own piece rates for weaving and designed his own layouts for mill machinery.

Young J.K. concluded that his uncle had a sixth sense that sometimes saved his companies from loss or disaster: "He seemed to know what people around him were thinking before they spoke and he had an ability to anticipate coming events that, to me, was uncanny." An example was the financial panic of 1907 when many of the nation's leading banks failed, and bankruptcies swept through American industry. Frank had prepared well in advance, so that his mills weathered the storm, survived a rash of cancelled orders, and had just enough work to keep his employees busy.

The most telling lesson that J.K. took from his uncle became a hallmark of his own career and of the later family business. It was Frank's conviction, frequently expressed, that "success meant an infinite care and attention to detail, something that can only be done in a single unit of business, with the boss constantly on the job."

As his nephew recalled it, Frank gave little indication that he wished to accumulate a fortune, but others in New Bedford saw it differently. His friend William W. Crapo, the lawyer who helped to finance Frank Knowles, once told J.K.: "Your grandfather Joe Knowles always wanted to do right. You know his son Frank very well. The difference was that Frank not only meant to do the right thing, but he meant to make a little money doing it."

J.K. had spent two years under the tutelage of his uncle at Hathaway before circumstance and his uncle's generosity and foresight gave young Milliken the opportunity of a lifetime.

In 1901, at the death of Jeddy Knowles, Frank came into his share of the substantial fortune of his parents. In the twenty-five years since the death of his father, thanks to Frank's management, his mother's one-third share was worth much more than the original estate in its entirety and she and other heirs had lived well in the interim. With fresh capital at hand he was prepared to launch the Mount Hope Finishing Company, assuming new risks and hoping for substantial rewards.

Frank Knowles lived to see the young firm beginning to prosper, even through the panic of 1907, but he died two years later at the age of fifty-six, the victim of a heart attack. J.K. felt a keen sense of loss at the passing of his counsellor and surrogate father. "I had reached the not very mature age of 34, and I could no longer have his help and advice. I must go it alone." In his old age, J.K. was to write of his Uncle Frank, who had given him such stern tutelage: "I have known a great many able and honest men. I have never known anyone who outranks him in these attributes."

"He went to the plant on Sundays"

✥ Young J.K. Milliken's success at Mount Hope won the attention of business and financial leaders of Massachusetts. He became a director—and later president—of the Machinists Bank of Taunton, and in 1912 was named to the board of Massachusetts Mutual Life Insurance Company, a post he was to hold for more than forty years.

The finishing plant grew steadily under J.K.'s unflagging attention. Its receipts in 1910 set a record of over $600,000, almost double those of 1909. The announced profit of $47,000 hinted that J.K. favored the conservative accounting principles used by Frank Knowles.

In that year J.K.'s family moved to the adjoining town of Taunton, where they were to live for more than a decade before returning to North Dighton. He drove the four miles to the plant, often at high speed in his big Buick roadster, and was usually among the first to arrive at the plant and the last to leave. He had begun the process of developing the village itself, an almost endless series of concerns that was to end in his patriarchal control of North Dighton. For the benefit of Mount Hope he developed streets and roads, prodded the state to remove rocks from the Three Mile River in the vain hope of barging in coal, and financed the power system. In addition he expanded the plant's water supply at every opportunity until the rights extended through streams and ponds for twenty-five miles or more, as far distant as Foxboro.

In 1913, on the eve of the outbreak of World War I, J.K. and Carrie went to Europe with other textile leaders and their wives. While there, the astute Milliken saw an opportunity and took prompt action. Sensing the approach of war and the resulting scarcity of dyes from Germany, he bought huge quantities of the best German dyes and had them shipped home where they literally filled the large cellar of his plant. Within months they were soaring in price, and for the next year and a half, so he reported to the Treasury Department, he sold a portion of these dyes at "a very handsome margin" and used the rest in his own plant at a time when they were not available to his competitors.

About this time, in 1914, J.K. played a leading role in founding the National Association of Finishers of Textile Fabrics, which was formed to help solve the industry's problems. Chief among the problems was that of stretched cloth, a phenomenon that stirred animosity between manufacturer and finisher. It was not unusual for cotton cloth to stretch as much as 10 percent during finishing, and Mount Hope frequently returned to customers about 107 percent of the goods sent in for processing. Milliken led a fight to keep for himself all goods over the guaranteed yardage and won a decision in the courts. The national association played a role in this victory.*

*First reference to an American trade association of textile finishers is dated 1898. J.K. Milliken was a member of this informal group of individuals.

In 1914, the informal group developed into the National Association of Finishers of Textile Fabrics. Its first officers were President John Bancroft, Joseph Bancroft & Sons; Chairman of Executive Committee Henry B. Thompson, United States Finishing Co.; Executive Committee Members Spencer Borden, Fall River Bleachery; J.K. Milliken, Mount Hope Finishing Co.; John Manley, Glenlion Dye Works and Sayles Bleachery; and Taylor Gause, Joseph Bancroft & Sons.

Robert D. Milliken was welcomed as a new member of the Executive Committee on September 18, 1963, at the Waldorf-Astoria, New York City, by Association President Ernest J. Chornyei.

The National Association of Finishers of Textile Fabrics was merged into the American Textile Manufacturers' Association in 1965. The last membership roll published prior to the merger with A.T.M.A. listed the following firms: Aurora Bleachery, Aurora, Ill.; Bradford Dyeing Association, Bradford, R.I.; Clearwater Finishing Co., Clearwater, S.C.; Cluett, Peabody & Co., Waterford, N.Y.; Cold Spring Bleachery, Yardley, Pa.;

In 1916 Mount Hope's receipts soared to $1,659,000, slightly more than the total investment in plant to that time. For the next year, 1917, income nearly doubled and was to climb steadily until the onset of the Great Depression.

The European tour had a tragic result for the Milliken family. Carrie contracted influenza or a similar illness, from which she was not to recover; she developed tuberculosis and was an invalid for years. J.K. continued to spend most of his time in the finishing plant, even on Sundays when he took Bob and Pete. The boys played among the machinery and wandered through the huge rooms while their father read his mail and studied incoming orders. Except for summer vacations these Sundays gave Bob and Pete their only familiarity with the plant in their boyhood. Because of Carrie's ill health the children went off to school, the boys as five-day boarders at Moses Brown and Helen to Wheeler's in Prov-

---

Commander Bleachery & Mfg. Co., Sand Springs, Okla.; Cranston Print Works, Cranston, R.I., Webster, Mass., Fletcher, N.C.; Crystal Springs Bleachery, Chickamauga, Ga.; Davis Mills Corp., Fall River, Mass.; Defiance Bleachery, Barrowsville, Mass.; Dodgeville Finishing Co., Attleboro, Mass., Blacksburg, S.C.; Exeter Mfg. Co., Exeter, N.H.; Fulton Finishing Division, Fulton Cotton Mills, Atlanta, Ga.; Harodite Finishing Co., North Dighton, Mass.; Indian Head Mills, Bancroft-Wilmington Division, Wilmington, Del., Bancroft-Arnold Division, Adams, Mass., Waldrich Division, Delawanna, N.J.; Lanett Bleachery & Dye Works, Lanett, Alabama; Lyman Printing and Finishing Co., Lyman, S.C.; Mansfield Bleachery, Mansfield, Mass.; Millville Mfg. Co., Manantico Bleachery and Dye Works, Millville, N.J.; Mount Hope Finishing Co., Butner, N.C.; North Carolina Finishing Co., Salisbury, N.C.; Pepperell Mfg. Co., Lewiston Division, Lewiston, Me., Finishing Plant, Pepperell, Ala.; Reeves Brothers, Inc., Fairforest Finishing Division, Spartanburg, S.C., Eagle & Phenix Division, Columbus, Ga.; Renfrew Bleachery, Unit of Abney Mills, Travelers Rest, S.C.; Rock Hill Printing & Finishing Co., Rock Hill, S.C.; Russell Mfg. Co. (Bleachery Div.), Alexander City, Ala.; Sayles Biltmore Bleacherys, Biltmore, N.C.; St. Louis Finishing Co., St. Louis, Mo.; Southern Bleachery & Print Works, Taylors, S.C.; Spring Cotton Mills, Grace Bleachery, Grace, S.C.; and Thomaston Mills (Bleachery Div.), Thomaston, Ga.

Lincoln Avenue Dam, North Dighton, 1918.

idence. Ruth attended The House in the Pines in Norton, a school recently founded by young Gertrude Cornish, who was to become J.K.'s second wife.

World War I brought a vast expansion of Mount Hope's business as New England mills flourished on government contracts, and the North Dighton plant worked at full speed to finish the goods. By the war's end, the Treasury Department estimated, on the basis of reported profits, that Mount Hope's stock was worth $1,250 per share—an estimate J.K. challenged as being almost 100 percent too high.

At this point, using war-time profits, J.K. began a five-year program of rebuilding the town. Old houses were moved in order to create a town park in front of the plant; old tenements were restored, and some two hundred new housing units were built for

Cooperative stores, North Dighton.

employees, most of them pleasant single-family dwellings set amid
large lawns. The new houses were complete with steam heat provided by coal-fired furnaces, full baths, hardwood floors and ample
storage space. Rents ranged from $1.25 to $3 weekly, at a time
when the average salary for workers was from $40 to $50 weekly.
During this period of progress the plant itself became more prosperous with each passing season. Except for a brief recession in
1921–22, the post-war boom was to roar on for almost ten years.

In 1922 Mount Hope entered a new era of technical advances
that was to give the company added advantages over competitors
and set a pattern for future development. The new day dawned
rather unpromisingly with the arrival of Douglas Robertson, a
towering, bony ex-army captain, recently discharged after duty
with the Ordnance Corps in France. A gifted engineer whose

talents were not yet obvious, Robertson was the son of a Canadian inventor who had migrated to Massachusetts some years earlier. The youngster had graduated from M.I.T. and worked briefly for the Remington Arms Company before joining the Army. Mount Hope's acquisition of the fledgling engineer was due to a quirk of familial pride. Doug Robertson had been operating a small foundry in Taunton, from which he returned home each evening with his clothing in sooty ruins. His father-in-law, who was something of a fashion plate, once accosted his friend J.K. Milliken, "Don't you need an engineer? Doug needs some kind of job that won't bring him home looking like a charcoal burner every night." Young Robertson reported for duty at Mount Hope a few days later.

J.K. appeared to have only the vaguest notion as to what Doug's duties should be. He sent the new engineer to report to a Portuguese foreman who knew even less of what was to be done with the unexpected recruit. As a result, Robertson remembered, "I wandered about, looking to see if there was something I could improve. The foreman never passed me an order. He never said much of anything."

The first of Doug's accomplishments sped the finishing process, with an improvement in profitability. J.K.'s announcement of his gratification was tinged with surprise. Robertson had begun a methodical study of the plant, concentrating first on the kiers, enormous pressure vats in which cloth was boiled in a solution of caustic soda for twelve hours. These kiers, fifteen feet in diameter and thirty feet deep, were laboriously filled with cloth by men who climbed inside and descended to the bottom where they worked for hours to pile the cloth into position for proper bleaching. The work was dangerous. One workman had narrowly escaped death by suffocation and another had been killed some years before when he was accidentally shut up inside a kier and had been boiled away in the caustic liquid. Doug revolutionized the process by introducing a cloth piling machine developed by one of his friends and making it more effective by installing an overhead track that moved the

Mount Hope Finishing Company, North Dighton, circa 1918.

device from kier to kier. Thereafter, Mount Hope's cloth was piled effectively by machinery, eliminating the dangerous and unpleasant task of hand piling.

Still Doug was not content. Kier bleaching struck him as wasteful in its use of vast quantities of soda solution, which was used once and discarded. Doug sent a sample of the used solution to the company laboratory for analysis and learned that the solution was still potent and therefore useful. He then developed a closed system of pipes to recirculate the solution, making possible the reuse of the liquor for a week's operation, all at the cost of a modest investment in a new piping system. This improvement saved Mount Hope $50,000 in its first year of operation and won J.K.'s rapt attention. This was merely the first of Doug Robertson's innovations that were to become familiar in the world's textile plants.

Robertson's most significant contribution to Mount Hope's prog-

Unloading bales.

ress and profitability came as the product of a happy accident. Bill Staples, the plant's finishing superintendent, had developed a new finish marquisette known as "puffy dots." The fabric, which was soon to take the curtain trade by storm, consisted of small raised circles of roving over a ground of the sheer cloth—a pattern of small dots. Staples had the threads of the dots sheared off and was attempting to fluff them out into tiny mounds. Until Robertson's arrival every experimental process used had left the dots mashed into a flat, unattractive pattern. To prevent the mashing of the dots, Robertson first devised an open mesh and then placed a blower beneath the moving cloth, hoping to dry it before it passed onto the tenter frame. To his surprise, the dots of roving blossomed out into "big, round, beautiful dots." The device was patented, and the handsome new curtain material finished by Mount Hope was

Cotton dye house.

on its way to a smashing market success that spanned a generation and showered profits not only on Mount Hope, but on several of its customers as well.

Doug Robertson was to remain at Mount Hope for fifteen years or more, developing more efficient machinery in many phases of company operations, all the while acting as a virtually independent agent, quite outside the hierarchy of the plant, and reporting directly to J.K. Some of his cohorts found his humorless, rather rigid military-style approach irritating, but there was no doubt of his ingenuity and his value to the company. He retained J.K.'s confidence and friendship. When Doug left the plant long afterward, at the approach of World War II, it was to become an industrialist on his own. J.K. told his departing engineer, "You'll never be happy with this mundane business of pushing goods through the plant. Machinery is your love and your talent, and you should be making it for yourself." J.K. gave Doug the Mount Hope patents he had developed during his employment, and in addition gave him American rights to manufacture a valuable French weft straightener which the firm had acquired. Robertson's new enterprise, Mount Hope Machinery, was independent of the Milliken firm and was a success from the start. Doug never forgot J.K.'s gift of the patents: "He was always one of the most generous managers in the entire industry, so far as his employees were concerned, and he was certainly that to me."

Doug's association with Mount Hope also brought about a long and mutually profitable association between his brother Stuart and the company. Stuart had worked for Mount Hope for a week or so in his youth before embarking on a profitable career as a manufacturer of curtains. Stuart's firm, Robertson Factories, was to become one of the most important customers of Mount Hope over many years and played a key role in J.K.'s development as a merchant banker.

⧉ At about the time of Doug Robertson's arrival in 1922, J.K. began to develop the most enduring political ties of his career. His friend Joseph W. Martin of North Attleboro, a young newspaper publisher who had already served in the Massachusetts legislature, asked J.K.'s help in a race for Congress. Milliken was enthusiastic, but discovered a formidable obstacle in Bob Leach of Taunton, a stove manufacturer who also aspired to the House seat for the district. J.K. worked out a compromise with the well-known and influential Leach: in return for Milliken's support, Leach would serve one term in the House and then back Joe Martin as his successor. The bargain was struck, and Martin campaigned for Congress in 1924 with J.K. furnishing substantial support. Though he was defeated in a close race, Martin reached his goal; his opponent died suddenly, and Joe was in Congress six months later. He took his seat in January, 1925.

Thus began Martin's long and distinguished congressional career as a conservative Republican spokesman, during which he worked with J.K. Milliken on a variety of political and economic issues. On his way to becoming minority floor leader and Speaker of the U.S. House of Representatives, Martin was generously supported by J.K., and in return the congressman exerted his growing influence to aid the Massachusetts textile industry on such issues as the maintenance of high tariffs on imported cotton and woolen products and matters of taxation and other concerns of general interest to New England industry. Martin's newspapers were also friendly to Mount Hope and its management.

Martin was an independent spirit in a mold J.K. could admire. He had become publisher of the North Attleboro *Evening Chronicle* at the age of twenty-four, bought out the partner who had financed the acquisition, then acquired a second paper in a nearby town to become an influential voice in public affairs of the region.

The rumpled figure of Joe Martin became increasingly familiar in North Dighton. The paunchy, balding congressman managed to look as if he slept in his clothes. His thinning hair was always in disarray, and his high-topped black shoes were habitually untied. To his constituents, he was a reassuring, intensely human voice of Washington political power, and his dimpled smile was unfailingly warm and ingratiating. His regular visits to J.K. bespoke their long, intimate association, and it was perhaps because of Martin that J.K. maintained the perennial interest in G.O.P. national politics which had been his birthright. Milliken never failed to contribute generously to the national Republican party, even during the long years of its trial as a minority party.

Another of J.K.'s intimate friends of this period was Bishop Cassidy of the local diocese, a moralist who was celebrated among the town's young people for his dedicated patrolling of a Dighton cemetery, during which he carried a stout stick with which to rout lovers. The bishop made frequent calls to J.K.'s office, where the old friends talked at length, often for hours, in the midst of Milliken's

United States dye house.

business day. Some of the plant's more cynical employees concluded that since many Mount Hope workers were Catholic, J.K.
felt that their attitudes might be influenced in some way by the
good bishop.

J.K. revealed a lack of partiality in religious matters. Though he
leaned to the Unitarian Church to which his forebears had turned
after deserting Puritanism, he was not a church-goer. As sales
manager Al Curt said when he was queried about J.K.'s religion,
"He went to the plant on Sundays." In his unheralded philanthropies, J.K. included all local churches and provided support to them
in a variety of ways, always on a basis of confidentiality.

A number of industrialists were among J.K.'s visitors, one of the
most colorful of whom was Walter Langshaw of New Bedford, a

Doubling and winding machine.

maverick English mill owner who kept the region in a turmoil with his unorthodox views of management. Other textile operators were outraged by Langshaw's charges of corruption, inefficiency and nepotism, which he said doomed the industry in New Bedford and Fall River. It was said that only J.K. could calm the obstreperous Langshaw, who would often stride into Milliken's office, roaring at the top of his voice, only to subside in J.K.'s presence and remain for long conversations in such a low voice that plant eavesdroppers heard nothing of his current philippic.

The mid-twenties brought a new phase in the succession of Mount Hope management. J.K. was in his prime and was to retain control for another quarter-century, but he now brought his sons into the business to prepare for carrying on the family tradition into a new generation. Pete was the first to work on a full-time basis, in 1924. He completed prep school and told his father that he preferred to work rather than enter college: "I'd only learn how to drink liquor more gracefully. I know what I'm supposed to do in my lifetime of work, and I want to get on with it. Why don't I get started?" As Pete recalled that interview, "Father thought I was crazy, but that I would change my mind." He went to work immediately, in the familiar surroundings he and Bob had known since early childhood. Both had worked in a variety of jobs during the summers since their teens, but, as Pete said, "There was never a discussion of our careers. We just assumed we'd go into the plant. It came naturally that we would enter the business."

Pete felt that his father had directed the supervisors with whom the boy worked to see that he was granted no favors, "in hopes that I would get over my feelings about college." It was to no avail. Pete had begun the work of his life and was to remain in the plant for more than twenty-five years, rising to become general superintendent. He became identified with the workers from the start with his friendly, democratic ways. As a friend remembered these years: "Pete played softball and baseball with the boys. He liked to ride the trucks and the fire engine, and was one of the gang. . . . He would get down and help the men do the dirty work, too."

Pete mastered the plant's machinery in methodical fashion: "I was never content to learn how to operate a machine. I kept on until I thought I wasn't inferior as an operator on any machine in that plant. People appreciate that sort of supervision, I think. Father did the same. Whenever anything went wrong, he was right down there." As a result of this attitude, Pete became an expert, capable of overseeing plant operations. He was also attuned to the less obvious ingredients of Mount Hope's success—especially to roles of the workers who tended machines. Pete saw in them practical observers whose advice was priceless: "Our supervisory group was responsive to suggestions from men who were working on the next step down—and that taught fellows on that level to take advice from everybody in the plant who had a suggestion. We had to listen to them automatically, whatever they had to say, and this became a never-ending source of change and improvements you could never think of yourself. I give those machine operators full credit. Those on the line got ideas much quicker than we did."

Bob Milliken, who graduated from Harvard in 1925, followed quite another route. His career was delayed for a year or more while he accompanied his mother to Asheville, North Carolina, in quest of a cure for her tuberculosis; Bob supervised purchase of a lot near that city and the building of a house, where Mrs. J.K. Milliken lived, under care of a nurse and chauffeur. She died in 1933 in North Dighton. Bob spent a year in an outside textile plant and joined Mount Hope in 1928, working at "a little of everything except the night shift." He soon found his calling in sales and finance, selling in Boston and New York and developing important customers. One of these was Robert Stone of Boston, of the Harvard class of 1922, who began modestly as a converter and became a manufacturer; he had most of his goods finished at Mount Hope.

Bob soon became a regular on the run to and from New York. He caught the night boat of the Fall River Line to New York, which docked downtown near the heart of the textile industry in the city of that era. Mount Hope's New York sales office was nearby, and Bob became a familiar figure there, an exuberant participant in the Jazz Age, given to wearing a raccoon coat, driving fast automobiles, and playing cards and dining out with the sales staff. These were boom times, and business was good at Mount Hope. Bob shared in the prosperity as a successful salesman but did not spend all his time in New York, returning to North Dighton each Thursday night. His weekends were not devoted to the plant's affairs.

Bob began fishing at the age of twelve, and hunting two years later. His tutor was A.I. Ballou who was in charge of Mount Hope's garage, where the company's fleet of Pierce Arrow trucks was housed. Ballou made Bob into an inveterate outdoorsman. They took frequent trips to Maine and Canada, and Bob kept both hunting dogs and horses in North Dighton. His enthusiasm extended to ice fishing in the bitter winters, in which he was occasionally joined by employees. He also formed a fishing and hunting club whose annual game dinners drew crowds of about 250 members, each bringing a contribution for the table.

Bob was married in 1932. His bride was Jean Thomas, the daughter of a Taunton stove manufacturer. They had been friends and neighbors since childhood, and the personable young Mrs. Milliken was to play an important role in Mount Hope affairs. As an unofficial diplomat she was notably effective in improving relations with company employees and customers. She was resigned to the demanding schedule followed by her husband—who spent every other week in New York from the start of their marriage. "Textile wives don't have easy lives," she said. "We learn to adapt." Bob's sister Helen, who had married Gordon Hughes, an M.I.T. graduate from Taunton, died soon after Bob and Jean had married, and the young couple took a great interest in the Hughes children, Bill, Polly and Betsy.

Bob's younger sister, Ruth, was beginning a career of her own. After graduating third in her Bryn Mawr class, she took graduate work at Oxford University, where she met and married Joseph F. FitzGerald, a Rhodes Scholar from Montana who was studying law. FitzGerald later represented the Civil Aeronautics Board in Alaska. He became president of Ozark Airlines, and they now make their home in Montana.

In the late twenties and early thirties, Mount Hope faced a technical challenge in the race to control the shrinkage of cloth. The challenge persisted for many years, and though J.K. was not the victor, he endured, and his plant continued to flourish. His adversary was Sanford Cluett, the inventor of Sanforization.

The textile industry of the post-war era was profoundly affected by the coming of Sanforization, the invention of the brilliant engineer Sanford Cluett, of Cluett, Peabody. Shrinkage, the bane of the consumer's existence, was brought under control for the first time.

Virtually the entire industry sought licenses under the Sanforization patent. Mount Hope, however, was one of the few firms to resist. Its engineers undertook the task of matching Cluett's results without infringing upon his patent, a process that was to continue for years. Mount Hope's refusal to accept Cluett's superiority was to be costly, but the Millikens never wavered. Pete explained, "We wouldn't put ourselves at Cluett's mercy. We didn't know what royalties might be tomorrow, and we didn't want to lose our identity, either."

In addition, Mount Hope did not wish to embark on a major program of advertising and promotion such as Cluett launched on behalf of Sanforization, which made possible the success of such licensees as the manufacturers of Arrow Shirts. J.K. hoped to solve the problem through the ingenuity of plant engineers and mechanics. The process they developed was called Wat-A-Set, which was used and promoted for a number of years—but, as Pete conceded, it was remarkably like the patented Cluett process. Mount Hope did learn a great deal about the technique of Sanforization from Al Carr, one of its employees who worked in the Cluett plant and studied the machinery involved. Cluett's process, it seemed, was the only way in which cloth could be successfully shrunk by mechanical means. His method was to pass cloth over a roller that was covered by an open blanket. The cloth passed straight down off the roller, the blanket reversed direction and closed, and the damp cloth, passing between blanket and roller, was dried in that position.

The Wat-A-Set method was so nearly identical that Cluett threatened suit but failed to press the matter. Sanforization long outlasted Wat-A-Set, which had served its purpose for Mount Hope by the 1960's and became obsolete with the advent of new fabrics. A long struggle had ended, in which there were charges of spying and counter-spying and backstage controversies between the principals. Long after the battle ended, Pete Milliken made a candid acknowledgment, "Wat-A-Set wasn't as good as the Cluett process, not even when we developed Wat-A-Set Elite. It couldn't have been. Cluett's accomplishment used the only mechanical process possible."

⟡ The depression of the early thirties, which opened with the stock market crash of October, 1929, found Mount Hope in condition to withstand severe adversity. As usual, the firm was debt-free. Though volume declined from a record $5,000,000 in 1925, receipts in 1929 were more than $3,000,000 and profits were $550,000. Volume declined slowly over the next four years, but the profit of $159,000 in the deflated economy of 1933 was not inconsiderable. The company's recovery was to be steady and sure. As yet there was no threat of labor trouble.

The first great wave of labor unrest in the textile industry devastated New England at large but left Mount Hope unscathed. The plant had grown remarkably in the past decade, but J.K. still seemed to know most of the workers by name, and the company's traditionally close personal relationships were reflected in strong anti-union sentiment among the workers. J.K.'s wage policy at this period was to pay the Fall River scale plus ten cents an hour coupled with numerous fringe benefits.

By August, 1928, a fifteen-week strike had virtually paralyzed New Bedford, "the aristocrat of American mill cities." The strike had been precipitated by a wage cut of 10 percent in response to poor business conditions caused by growing competition and overproduction stimulated by World War I. Since the average mill worker's salary was about $19 a week, the cut reduced thousands of families to sub-marginal levels, and the infant United Textile Workers Union moved in. Though it could muster only forty thousand members among the million or more American textile workers, it soon immobilized both New Bedford and Fall River.

A visiting reporter from the *Baltimore Sun* concluded that the real villain in the strike was the rising south, which had been claiming New England mills for many years: "Newer mills with better machinery, closer proximity to raw material, cheaper power, lower taxes and cheaper labor are underselling New England mills and yet making a profit. The cotton manufacturing business in

New England is simply being strangled to death and mill owners and mill workers alike are suffering."

But though Mount Hope's volume had fallen by some 20 percent from its post-war peak, the firm was still busy and profitable. Receipts for 1928 were over $3,500,000, and profits exceeded $530,000. J.K. was not yet alarmed despite his realization that an increasing share of his business was coming from southern mills, which entailed higher transportation costs. Unless the trend worsened the future of Mount Hope in New England seemed bright, since the plant's quality control standards and prompt service continued to give it an advantage over competitors.

By 1934, as the nation struggled in the depression, the plant's volume was still around $3,000,000, but profits dwindled to $187,000—and would plunge to $87,000 the following year. The general strike of 1934, which once more gripped New Bedford and Fall River textile plants, brought a sterner test for Mount Hope, which was the only large non-union plant in the region—and a tempting prize to union leaders. The United Textile Workers, now led by the aggressive British-born Francis Gorman, had marked J.K.'s busy plant as a special target and drew plans to invade its model village. These plans, of course, posed a direct threat to Mount Hope, whose business was already being affected by strikes against its customers, the cotton manufacturers.

The able and resourceful Gorman, who had called out fifty thousand across the U.S., charged that northern manufacturers had encouraged the strike, hoping to spread unionism to the south. But though the strike dragged on for months and more than forty thousand state troops had been mustered to keep peace, this offensive had also failed. Gorman's goals had been a 33 percent rise in wages and a reduction of the work week to thirty hours. In city after city, settlements dashed the hopes of workers. In New Bedford threats of kidnapping were made against the families of mill owners, and mobs roamed streets at night, smashing windows with stones. After several days of violence J.K. and his sons heard rumors that the irate strikers planned an invasion of North Dighton, to be led by "Ann The Red" Berlach and another radical organizer, Mariano Bishop.

To augment the inadequate local police force of three men, the Millikens deputized forty to fifty employees, who armed themselves with clubs and pistols. Every street leading into the village was barricaded with piles of sandbags and each entrance was manned by armed guards based in small guard houses that looked for all the world like privies. J.K. had called in Tim Manning of Providence, Rhode Island, a specialist in the recruiting of private police forces and strike breakers. Manning imported about twenty guards from New York or New Jersey, rough-looking men who seemed more menacing to Jean Milliken and other women of the town than the prospect of an invasion by strikers. Guards with shotguns were posted around the home of the Millikens, some of them farmers who came from the outlying areas as volunteers.

The town and the plant waited tensely for two or three weeks but the crisis passed without violence. Bands of strikers appeared at the barricades now and then but turned back after a few moments of shouting and milling about. Police Chief Jack Synan made only one arrest, when a van was passed through a barricade and broke down. A search revealed men hiding within, among them the organizer Mariano Bishop, who was charged with trespass; the driver was charged with transporting passengers without a license, and the intruders were hustled out of town. The plant continued to run at its normal pace, and workers clung to their anti-union attitudes. As Harry Corr recalled it, "The people of North Dighton did more to turn back the mob of strikers than the New York goons. All the help was on J.K.'s side. They wanted no part of unions in those days."

The threat receded, but J.K. and his sons resolved that they would be prepared for the next crisis. Until now the town had spent from $2,500 to $3,000 annually on its police force, with most of the cost borne by Mount Hope. The plant now made a substantial gift to the town government—it was reported to be about $10,000—to create an adequate police force. A reporter from the New Bedford *Standard* wrote in early January, 1935: "Dighton abounds with police officers, one for every 30 of the town's inhabitants. Special forces drill with rifles and bayonets for any emergency. . . . It is the best-policed community in Massachusetts today, numerically speaking." He found a force of 114 men, 23 of them regular policemen, supported by a reserve of 86 carefully chosen local citizens.

Chief Synan observed that, "Even now in a town this size, there isn't ordinarily enough to keep four men busy. The work is mostly investigating accidents or someone reporting dogs raided his chicken yard. We're a quiet, law-abiding little community." He complained that the governor had refused to send militiamen to help guard the town when strikers threatened. "We couldn't get protection from the state police. Politics interfered there again. Now that the election is over you can get all the state police you want." Synan replied to widespread criticism of Mount Hope's preparations for a seige: "There was nothing left to do but what we did. We couldn't recruit the qualified men we needed. I was worried enough for fear some of my men might shoot themselves with their own guns. So we've decided to be ready for them the next time if there is another emergency."

The Mount Hope militia drilled faithfully for a few months, marching through the village streets daily, practicing maneuvers and bayonet drills on the school playground, and attending lectures on tactics on rainy days. The tiny army was organized completely, with officers and non-commissioned officers, a supply department, even a bugler. But drills became less frequent as time passed, members lost interest, and the town returned to normal.

"I'm no damned Lord!"

The approach of World War II found Mount Hope prosperous and its workers secure in their jobs and sheltered by a system of benefits which made the company a leader in New England industry. The plant and the village of North Dighton had become, for all practical purposes, a single entity.

The Mount Hope brand of paternalism, which J.K. and his family regarded as enlightened philanthropy, had few parallels in U.S. industry. The company reached into virtually every aspect of community life, for J.K. seemed to think of everything that would make for dedicated employees. The Mount Hope clubhouse (dues fifty cents monthly) had card rooms, a library, dances, theatricals, a basketball court and free showers. Bridge, whist, cribbage, dartball, billiards and pool were popular with members. A nearby theater showed silent movies, free except for a collection to pay the piano player.

A Mount Hope glee club gave concerts at home and on the road. There was a cooperative store organized by Englishmen who had brought the model from their own country; shoppers enjoyed low prices and participated in quarterly division of profits. A cooperative savings bank served the purpose of later credit unions, but there was no loan office, since J.K. felt that debts encouraged bad habits. If an employee needed some essential item—J.K. barred such luxuries as pianos or phonographs—he could borrow from Mount Hope without interest. The only recorded loss to the company during the life of this program occurred when an employee was permanently disabled in an accident.

Athletics were important the year around. Tom Hall, the athletic director, recruited college players, saw that they had part-time work in the plant and organized them into teams. The baseball team frequently lead the Eastern Industrial League and in 1920 won the title for teams east of the Mississippi. Employees supported the teams enthusiastically and rode to nearby games in company trucks. Excitement reached such a pitch that Bob O'Hara, the team's star, once climbed into the stands to punch a heckler, to the cheers of Mount Hope faithful. In later years, O'Hara went on to a successful career with a rival firm, Bancroft Finishing.

J.K. frowned on football as too dangerous but encouraged soccer, for which several star British players were recruited. Mount Hope basketball teams were also successful. Less strenuous recreation for all employees was provided; ski trains to New Hampshire usually carried at least five hundred employees and excursions to eastern Cape Cod for lobster bakes were equally popular.

Not content with the development program of the 1920's, J.K. added new housing for employees and encouraged home ownership. Workers living in rental units were urged not to overcrowd the houses and were moved when additional children arrived. Settled employees who wished to own their homes approached J.K., who sent them to an architect, donated the lot, dug the cellar and furnished foundation stone. Employees were sent to the local bank to finance the balance, but the company took second mortgages and permitted both mortgages to be paid in small weekly installments, so as to clear the debt in a maximum of twelve years.

The Millikens built homes for themselves about this time, and even J.K.'s large house, "Green Acres," did not seem a mansion by comparison with the homes of workers. J.K. was determined that North Dighton should have none of the look of a typical mill town filled with mean, cramped little tenements.

Householders were aided in many ways. Mount Hope mowed lawns, trimmed trees, raked leaves and cleared snow from streets, sold power, coal, firewood and water cheaply, and connected telephones to the local system without charge. All houses were repainted and papered every three years and though householders had no choice as to colors and patterns, they lived in fresh, clean surroundings.

The "picture postcard" town became a magnet to tourists. On Sunday afternoons a steady stream of automobiles from the area passed slowly through North Dighton, filled with admiring visitors. Important guests from abroad were frequently brought to the town to observe the economic and social aspects of the singular mill village. John Brooks, an English worker who had spent many years in the plant, said, "Our houses certainly didn't look like mill houses. They were new, too, and everything was well-kept. It was truly a model village, set in a beautiful landscape. It was heaven on earth in that town." As to the plant itself, as Brooks said, "You could eat off the floor."

Mount Hope subsidized the fire and police services and several churches as well. The large company farm produced milk, eggs and vegetables, which were delivered at cost to the homes of employees. The farm was a major enterprise, with a herd of one hundred Jersey and Holstein cows bred from championship stock, a flock of 2,500 hens, and one hundred pigs. In 1944 the farm produced a bumper potato crop of three thousand bushels. The hospital, one of J.K.'s continuing interests, was steadily improved. Two nurses and two assistants were always on duty, and a doctor was on call. Rates were kept to the minimum. The average cost of a stay in the maternity ward for mother and child was $25 during the late 1920's and early 1930's. More serious cases were sent to Boston hospitals, at Mount Hope's expense. A village visitor made regular calls to see that home conditions were good and advised on diets, sanitation and other household matters. Those with vegetable gardens received free seed and fertilizer.

Mount Hope News, the company's monthly house organ, made frequent mention of these benefits, urging employees to participate in all programs. The magazine was also given to moralistic epigrams: "Good will is the disposition of the customer to return to the place where he has been well treated.—U.S. Supreme Court," and "It's a great life if you don't weak-end."

There was no formal pension plan, but the natural anxieties of the workers were allayed somewhat by J.K.'s highly personal system of dealing with each retiring worker individually. Terms remained confidential, but a newspaper report of 1951 indicated that pensions of that era averaged about $100 a month, a generous level for the time.

Hard times worked few changes in working conditions at Mount Hope. The work week was normally stable unless business came to a virtual standstill. In 1936, when J.K. forecast a difficult first quarter for the coming year, he instituted a short-time schedule but set all employees to washing windows, scrubbing floors, chopping brush or mowing lawns, all at their usual rate of pay. In this way he tided them over a severe business slump, and only when the downturn continued into a second quarter did he order further cuts.

In this case he named a "budget committee" of Doug Robertson, Al Carr and Harry Bridgford and directed them to reduce the payroll to 55 percent of the billing, with the proviso that, if they failed, he would consider closing the plant. This entailed the unpleasant task of interviewing department heads and arguing as to which cuts should be made. It brought on a flurry of telephone calls to committee members from angry workers who were laid off temporarily, but the drastic remedy saw Mount Hope through the crisis, and full employment returned a few months afterward. These were temporary layoffs, and virtually the only ones during Mount Hope's first fifty years. Few workers were fired by the company. John Brooks said, "In all the years I worked there, I can recall only two people being fired—one who stripped lead from the plant roof to get money to buy liquor, and a truck driver who ran through a door and knocked down a woman employee."

🙧 By now, after almost forty years of the company's growth, J.K. and Mount Hope had become inseparable in the minds of his employees and friends, and his personality and character might well have been carried on the books as corporate assets. Milliken had become one of the best-known industrialists in New England, the acknowledged "dean of the finishing business," and a hero in the eyes of most of North Dighton's villagers who created an extensive folklore from his personal traits. They found him courteous and considerate, even compassionate, and over the years uncovered many instances of his anonymous benefactions to employees— acts of kindness usually effected through third parties. This reputation and his air of unruffled reserve made his eccentricities all the more appealing to watchful villagers.

Townspeople grew accustomed to seeing J.K. walk from his home to the plant early every morning at his brisk, erect stride, stooping now and then to pick up bits of paper and other litter, stuffing them into a pocket and dropping them into a waste can near the plant. Occasionally, when he drove to work, J.K. halted his car and got out to pick up trash from the village green. He once found an entire newspaper there, which he crumpled and burned on the spot. His example was not lost on loyal employees, many of whom emulated him and helped to preserve the spotless appearance of the town.

J.K.'s uncertain moods were a matter of importance to people in the plant, particularly to newcomers, who were tutored with care: "If he comes through with his hat brim turned up he's feeling good, and you can ask him anything. But if you see him in his office with his hat pulled down over his eyes, take care. Back out and postpone your mission."

Even in his most severe moods, however, J.K. usually displayed a sardonic humor that won over victims of his barbs. He was particularly sensitive to the criticism (which was seldom voiced) that he ruled his barony of North Dighton like a benevolently autocratic Olympian. He once bewildered a young salesman who innocently aroused his feelings on the subject. Fred Engels, a rather dashing newcomer to the New York office, visited J.K. in the plant one day, and as the two left the office to go into the plant young Engels held the door, bowed and said, "After you, My Lord."

J.K.'s roar echoed through the hall and nearby offices, "I'm no damned Lord!"

When they reached the street level, J.K. turned to his chauffeur, Coke Ballou, and said, "Take this bird to the State line and get rid of him."

Milliken's sense of humor was sometimes almost ceremonial; some of his cherished pleasantries were repeated for years. Anne Synan, who worked in the payroll office, went into J.K.'s office each pay day, carrying to him a pay envelope identical to those handed to all plant workers. Milliken went through the same charade each time. "Wait a minute, Doris," he said, confusing her with another woman employee, as usual. J.K. opened his little envelope and counted the bills into piles by denomination, then looked up with a wan smile, "Now isn't that a pittance? Not even cigar money, is it? Would you go downstairs and get another $300 for me?"

For years, Anne fretted over the plight of the plant owner who was so inadequately paid. It was much later when she realized what the extent of his earnings from dividends and other sources must have been.

Al Curt of the New York office felt that J.K.'s humorous sallies often cloaked his real meaning. The old man visited the New York sales staff so infrequently that Curt once asked him if he disliked the city. "Yes!" J.K. said. "And I'll tell you why. The water in these darned hotels isn't cold enough for my morning shower."

For all J.K.'s lifelong habit of attention to detail, he was in some respects notably absentminded. He visited Albert Carr's office when he had run out of cigars, and asked brightly, "You got a cigar, Al?" Carr never smoked cigars but soon learned to keep them on hand. J.K. apparently never realized that he was imposing upon his involuntary tobacconist. As Carr recalled, J.K. would bum one cigar and them rumble amiably, "Gimme a handful of 'em, Al," and walk away with a cigar clamped firmly between his teeth, trailing a cloud of smoke.

Though he was seldom without a cigar, J.K. realized that smoking was a bad habit and offered his sons $1,000 rewards if they reached age twenty-one without smoking. Bob won—and made the same offer to his children in turn. J.K.'s offer was typical of his rather distant relationship with his sons. J.K.'s devotion to business dictated these relationships. He seemed to be baffled as to the cause of this, but it may have stemmed from his tenuous relationship with his own father, of whom he saw little. At the time of his father's death, he took Bob to the funeral in Farmington, Maine, but the boys knew little else of their paternal grandfather.

Albert Curt, to whom J.K. had been a sort of foster father, often heard J.K. hint of his failure as a parent. "I have always been able to do more with you and for you than I could with my own sons," the old man said. And Pete Milliken, speaking of the relationship between J.K., Sr., and his mentor, Frank Knowles, said, "He had more of a father-son relationship with his uncle that he ever established with his own sons."

But J.K. was obviously proud of his sons. He once told Albert Carr: "Those two are so different. I'm a lucky man. They fit into our situation so well. Pete handles people well, and Bob handles money well; he really knows the value of a dollar." Even in their earliest years, J.K. found little time to enjoy the company of his sons. As Pete recalled, "He was never at home, early or late—always at the plant, or elsewhere on business." Occasionally in the first years of his fatherhood, as he prepared to mount his horse for the ride to the plant, Milliken would lift young Bob and Pete to the animal's back and ride with them a few yards to the edge of the property, where the boys would slide off, and watch their father disappear in the direction of the plant.

By a coincidence, horseback riding also provided a bond between J.K. and Bob's future wife. Jean Thomas, who was also a riding

enthusiast from youth, frequently rode with J.K. and his daughter
Ruth over North Dighton trails. The youngster who was to marry
Bob never forgot those occasions. "He would invite me to ride with
him, and set a definite hour, of course. So I would report to the
plant promptly, and almost invariably he would keep me waiting,
for an hour or an hour and a half—quite a long time for such a
little girl as I was, waiting on a hard wooden bench."

It was not unusual for J.K. to lose himself in the details of his
business affairs, and on occasion he became sublimely indifferent
to all else. One day, during the latter years of his life, Jean Milliken
sent her young son Jake the two hundred yards from her home to
J.K.'s house with some papers for his grandfather. When the boy
returned Mrs. Milliken asked, "What did he say?" Jake reported
casually, "He didn't say nothin' and I didn't say nothin'."

J.K.'s Mount Hope staff, however, found him ever alert and
attentive to the least details in the life of the plant. For many years,
apparently from the start of the company, he held a morning
meeting of superintendents and foremen for a full discussion of
the day's orders, including the routing of cloth through the plant
and the treatment of each order. All complaints were presented
and examined from several points of view until he was content.
But, as Harry Corr recalled, the old man was always pragmatic:
"J.K. trained us damned well, and forgot nothing. If we were
looking for trouble with an order, for instance, and it turned out to
be some insignificant little stains, J.K. would say, 'If you have to get
a microscope to look at it, or stand on your head to see it, there's no
complaint.'" Otherwise, he would pursue trouble, or potential
trouble, to its source.

During his early days in the plant, Corr was a lot chaser. One day,
in his anxiety to get an order out of some department where it was
being held overlong, he was balked by the authority of a superintendent, Phil Lavoie, who refused to release the cloth. The slowdown soon became apparent to J.K., who called Corr into his office
and inquired what the trouble was. The brash youngster realized

that Lavoie could fire him at any moment, but he told J.K., "Phil Lavoie's the trouble. He won't give it to me."

J.K. then called in Lavoie and two or three other superintendents and asked Corr to repeat his story. "Phil won't give me what I need," Harry said. "So it's his fault. There was nothing I could do."

The brief confrontation settled the matter and re-established open channels in the plant. "From that day on, I was in solid," Corr recalled. Lavoie accepted the verdict, and the boy lot chaser was spared for a useful career with Mount Hope.

Everyone who knew him well apparently found J.K. courteous and considerate under most circumstances, but he left no one in doubt of his resolve to direct his own destiny and that of Mount Hope in the way he thought best. His cousin Eliot Knowles, who was much younger, judged J.K. on the basis of a close working relationship during the 1940's: "He was never a tyrant—more of an autocrat, I'd say. A tyrant wouldn't have provided a hospital and the other things he did. But he *was* an autocrat. People did things his way. When I was young, for example, our family always went to his house. He never came to ours. His brother Alf did come to see us, but not J.K."

A story about Alf Milliken as recalled by Mount Hope officials may have explained some of J.K.'s impatience with his brother. As a young Harvard alumnus, Alf had returned for a Yale football game, cheered his team to victory, and gone out with jubilant classmates to celebrate. He apparently knew nothing of the next twenty-four hours—until he regained consciousness in an empty freight car in the Harlem yards of New York City.

Whatever the truth of this tale, Eliot Knowles had a pleasant memory of Alf, who had joined Mount Hope after graduation: "He wasn't at all like J.K. Alf was a warm, outgoing man, full of stories, a bon vivant, rather fond of a dram. I got the feeling that J.K. never permitted Alf to do what he was capable of doing. Alf was the salesman and J.K. was the inside man in the early years. And Alf was one of the best salesmen, and one of the best guys, you can imagine. He often bought and sold grey goods, taking hedging positions, and was successful at it. He never seemed to win the acclaim of the other Millikens, but he was a genius at marketing."

J.K. and Alfred were not the only members of their family generation to win distinction. Their sister Grace, who was an artist in early life, decided, at age forty, to become a physician. She gave up painting, entered Tufts College, and was off on a medical career. She became a well-known doctor in Boston, where she practiced for many years.

In one respect J.K. lived a secret life of his own. He was remarried in 1935 after a courtship of which his family knew nothing; his bride was Gertrude Cornish, the schoolmistress of The House in the Pines, where his daughter Ruth had been a student. This happy union was to endure for the rest of J.K.'s life and work major changes in his outlook.

Though Gertrude took an active interest in his affairs and achieved close relationships with his family, she managed to break his routine of spending virtually all of his time at the plant. For the first time in his life, J.K. found himself enjoying opera and symphony concerts and taking active part in church activities. Gertrude also maintained her interest in education and served as trustee and benefactor of Middlebury College. It was only after her death that the Millikens discovered the tender love letters from J.K. revealing an unsuspected side of his nature in the expression of romantic love that bordered upon the poetic.

A vital element in the success of Mount Hope in this era was the development of the New York sales office, which had begun in the mid-1920's. At first J.K. had depended upon veteran sales representatives who had learned the trade with other firms, and until about 1925 his New York sales representative was James Brown, whose secretary was a North Dighton youngster, Freddie Knop. After a time Brown was dismissed and J.K. established an office on an expanded basis with Knop in charge. Two or three promising young men, usually from the Mount Hope work force, were sent to New York each year until J.K. discovered those who were most talented as salesmen. One of his discoveries was Albert Curt of the neighboring village of Somerset, the son of a French mother and a Portuguese father. Most of the members of the large Curt family had worked for Mount Hope, and Albert began on his sixteenth birthday.

After spending one day sweeping the floor, Curt became a lot chaser and was then given "the best job in the plant—sample boy." Albert was in charge of incoming cloth from the opened bale until it was finished, and since a sample from each lot must be taken to J.K. for approval, the boy soon came to know him: "I'd go to his door three or four times a day and stand until he told me to enter. J.K. would run his hands through the cloth and tell me to submit a sample to New York. Sometimes he would have his mail spread on the desk when I went in, and say, 'I wonder what we'll do with that,' just as if asking my advice."

Curt was almost eighteen when J.K. abruptly took notice of him one day and questioned him about his family. Absently fingering a sample, he said, "How'd you like to go to the New York office?"

"That's my ambition."

"Well, I wouldn't give a damn for a fellow without ambition, but you've got to have something else. How old are you?"

When Al confessed that he was only seventeen, J.K. said, "Oh, you're too young—but since I've got you all steamed up about it, talk it over with your folks and see how they feel."

Curt was jubilant. Despite the delights of a sample boy's life, he had tired of rising before dawn to catch a trolley for the 6:45 A.M. opening of the plant, which closed at 5:45 P.M.

His salary of $16 per week was raised to $35 when he was sent to the New York office at 66 Leonard Street. He prospered and saved money (his room rent was $4 weekly). In 1923, when his father died, Curt was advised by J.K. to return home and help his mother with the rearing of his eleven brothers and sisters. "When I got back to Dighton," Curt recalled, "I found $75 in my pay envelope. J.K. treated me like a son. He told me to work anywhere in the plant I liked, to learn the business." Within two years Curt was back in New York and became a salesman, urged by J.K. to "sharpen your teeth on some new customers." Curt was a success from the start in the highly competitive field.

At this promotion J.K. asked Curt's advice as to his successor and Al suggested Bob O'Hara, the baseball star, who was Al's elder. Curt recalled: "When someone called for a sample, I'd say, 'OK I'll send the boy up with it.' That night O'Hara got after me, 'You so and so, I'll do anything you ask me to—but don't you ever tell 'em again you're sending the boy!' "

Curt's customers soon learned to trust him: "I would never send them a sample. I'd take it myself, so that I was in contact with them practically every day—and if they had criticisms, they'd give them to me, and I'd write the plant in detail. I'd have every order sent to me on approval and then clear it with my customers." He soon developed customers, including Manhattan Shirts, into major accounts.

Even without J.K.'s tutelage Curt cared for his money from the start, aware that he was not guaranteed a pension at the end of his career. A few years later J.K. gave Curt a token three shares of Mount Hope stock and eventually placed him on the Board of Directors. As business grew, new men from Mount Hope's plant joined the New York office, until there were thirteen salesmen. Fred Knop was succeeded by Charles Hathaway and he in turn by Curt, who then had a dozen years' experience. "By that time," Curt recalled, "we really had no competition. Our service was superior and the trade knew it. We got the best of the business. Most customers were converters around New York, but I had an out of town man to cover Philadelphia, Chicago and St. Louis."

Mount Hope ran artificial shirtings in Curt's early years in New York and progressed to rayon piece goods for lingerie, then to acetates. Throughout, there was a large volume of marquisette curtain material in "puffy dots," as developed by Staples and Doug Robertson. As materials changed during the thirties, Mount Hope's chief competitors became U.S. Finishing, Sayles and Joseph Bancroft in New England, and Union Bleacheries in the south. Since the southward migration of textile plants had begun, Mount Hope was losing its advantage: "J.K. hung on for a long time after most mills had gone south," Curt recalled. "Fall River, which once had 135 mills, finally got down to none—a ghost town, so far as textiles went. J.K. competed with intelligent moves and short cuts—his use of the fleet of trucks in our region helped a lot."

By 1948 another promising sales chief had appeared in the New York office, also as a sample boy. He was Bobby Stegeman, a native New Yorker who came in occasionally as messenger boy for a textile firm. A personable youngster of seventeen, Stegeman was offered a job by Curt. Stegeman remembered: "I was making $120 a month at my old job, and Al offered to pay me weekly, just $30, but the difference meant something to me then." He was sent to North Dighton for a few months, at a salary of $40 per week, and wrote to Curt from North Dighton, asking if he might participate in the plant's bonus plan. Curt refused but had the boy raised to $80 per week. "I couldn't believe it," Stegeman recalled long afterward. "I ran to the cashier's office with my first check to get cash—and it wasn't half an hour before the whole plant knew that this fresh kid from the New York streets was making all this money. That was a lesson."

Upon his return to New York Stegeman began as a salesman, rapidly gaining a following among customers and learning the trade so thoroughly that he was to succeed Curt upon his retirement. "He became the best," Curt said. "He was the only man we hired from outside the plant in my day, but he learned so quickly. He didn't have to be told twice. He was a natural salesman." Stegeman was to find a special niche in Mount Hope's future.

The maturity of Mount Hope as a major factor in the American textile industry was due as much to J.K.'s financial genius as to his competence as a finisher. His gifts as a money handler were demonstrated in the rise of Robertson Factories in the late twenties. Stuart Robertson had become a seasoned veteran of the curtain trade when the owner of his firm, enriched through a stock market speculation, decided to sell out. With J.K.'s backing, and his use of "a gentle club" to persuade the owner, Robertson and a few other employees bought the company and Stuart was launched on his career.

When Stuart went to Mount Hope for help he found his brother Doug sitting with J.K. in his office. Stuart explained his need for capital and excitedly pictured the potential for large profits.

"How much do you need?" J.K. asked.

"Fifty thousand."

J.K. turned to Doug. "Shall we take a chance on him?"

"Well, he's my brother."

J.K. pointed a stubby finger at Doug. "All right, then. You're responsible. You keep your eye on that $50,000."

Milliken did not provide the money himself but established credit for Stuart at a bank, and a long, profitable collaboration began. Stuart expanded his plant with advances from J.K. and was then enabled to buy out his partners and build Robertson Factories into the major curtain manufacturer in the U.S. From a modest beginning, J.K.'s advances to Stuart became enormous, all extended with no other security than the agreement that Mount Hope finish the goods Stuart produced.

But though they remained fast friends until Milliken's death, J.K. and Stuart conducted every transaction as if their lives and fortunes were at stake. If Mount Hope's price happened to be a fraction of a cent higher than the competition, Stuart would renegotiate and switch his business without hesitation. J.K. always found ways to win him back—most dramatically in the case of "puffy dot" curtains by offering Robertson exclusive rights to manufacture, an arrangement that enriched both firms for years. Long after J.K.'s death Stuart Robertson said of him, "I never knew a tougher, straighter, or kinder man to do business with. He'd take on Goliath. Absolutely fearless."

J.K. aided numerous textile manufacturers during their early years to the mutual advantage of the parties. He once advanced $1,500,000 to a customer with no other collateral than an agreement that Mount Hope would finish the customer's goods. Sales manager Albert Curt remembered Milliken's role in the success of Karl Robbins and his highly profitable mills: "A little fellow came in the New York office one day with a slip of paper in his hand and said his name was Robbins, and asked if we would finish some goods for him—just 2000 yards. I told him we'd be glad to do it, and we did.

"The orders from him came slowly but they grew, and J.K. took a liking to Robbins—a gentleman, he said. Robbins was one of the first to get into rayon and he began to make money and expand. After some time, he'd go up to Dighton with me and see J.K. and go through the plant. He would go home with me to dinner and my mother fed him franks and baked beans, and Robbins would say, 'Delicious!', and then add, inexplicably, 'God bless all the little children.' "

Once when he was visiting the plant, Robbins told J.K. he thought he would sell out. "Why?" J.K. asked. Robbins explained that he lacked the capital to improve his operations so as to make them truly profitable. When J.K. asked how much he needed, and Carl said about $100,000, J.K. said he'd lend it to him, "on his face." Robbins accepted, and that was only the beginning. "Many's the time I walked down Broadway with checks for Carl Robbins, for $200,000 to $300,000—who could have anything he wanted from J.K., just so long as we got the finishing.

"We went on for years together, getting bigger and bigger. Sometimes Carl would call from Hemp, down in North Carolina, and say, 'Curtie, I've got a note due at the bank tomorrow with Mr. Milliken. Will you please tell him I'm down here and can't get a check to him until Monday. But be sure you tell him. I don't want him to think I'd ever let him down.' "

There were other examples of such financing by J.K., in and out of the textile industry. One was Robert Stone, of Boston, one of Bob's Harvard friends who began as a converter in a small way, then became a manufacturer on his own and achieved marked success. Like Stuart Robertson he was a favored licensee of "puffy dot" curtains in his early career and profited in several ways from J.K.'s aid and sagacity.

J.K.'s kinsman Eliot Knowles, the grandson of Frank Knowles, now a New Bedford banker, had succeeded his father on the Mount Hope Board of Directors. Eliot regarded J.K. with a banker's eye and marveled at the finishing company: "It was a fantastically well-run outfit, financially. So far as I know he was never in debt. He always had an investment account, usually in government bonds. He didn't have to pay out much in dividends; during most of his career, income taxes were low. He was very careful of his earnings and did not distribute more than his family needed—and he knew the family's needs very well.

"He was a banker and played the game constantly, looking for opportunity. If he saw a chance to get the finishing of cloth he would get his hands on an enterprise through financing it. He looked in many directions. Since he used a lot of gas in the plant, he was interested in that. He tried to organize a gas utility, forming the Wanoat Gas Company, then trying to take over the Taunton Gas Company and the North Attleboro Gas Company, which would have formed a small utility. He failed in that. But he tried it in banking, too, with Bristol Trust Company; that one didn't work, either. But of course he had Dighton Transfer and another subsidiary, Dighton Factors."

ᐸᔑ World War II brought a new era of prosperity to Mount Hope, as it did to most American industry; most of the company's young men went into service, replaced by women and old men, but productivity remained high, and the company won an E Award for exceptional contributions to the war effort. J.K. was entering his late sixties, still vigorous and active, but he leaned heavily on Bob and Pete, who were now in fact the company's chief executives, working in their respective fields.

It was near the end of the war that the most controversial figure in Mount Hope history joined the firm. He was Frank Daylor, a balding, round-faced accountant who had begun his career as a locomotive fireman on the Boston-Taunton line and had now become a business consultant. As the former chief of the Internal Revenue office in Fall River, Daylor had become acquainted with J.K. and impressed him with his acumen and vigorous, creative approach to the problems of industry. The newcomer became J.K.'s most trusted counsellor during the company's time of trial and was soon so firmly entrenched as a Milliken family favorite that he was above criticism.

Irreverent observers maintained that Daylor's counsel had failed to help other troubled textile firms in the area, some of which had gone out of business. Eliot Knowles, who regarded him as a divisive influence at Mount Hope almost from the start, felt that Daylor might have had ambitions to take over control of Mount Hope. In any case, Daylor had access to J.K.'s "innermost thoughts," acted as his trusted lieutenant, and became increasingly influential in directing company policy. Until that time, Eliot Knowles recalled, things had gone well at Mount Hope, which was "such a well-run organization that things were well-nigh ideal. It was that way until Daylor came, during the war."

Daylor advised J.K. in many fields other than taxation. He was insistent that the plant should be sold and the business moved to the south to be near the majority of its customers, timely advice indeed. Daylor also urged a revision of the capital structure, beginning with the purchase of stock held by outside interests. J.K. gave his approval, and Mount Hope bought the shares owned by the Hathaway and Stanton families, which had been part of the corporation from its beginning.

The Milliken and Knowles families came to disagree over the value of Daylor's contributions—that, at least, was the memory of Knowles representatives on the board. Eliot Knowles recalled that Daylor became a factor in an increasingly acrimonious conflict between the closely related families that had founded the firm. George Knowles was the first victim of this dispute, unceremoniously forced from the Board of Directors in 1948. This left Eliot Knowles and Donald Hyde of New Bedford, an attorney representing the Crapo family interests, to oppose the Milliken majority on the Board: J.K. Milliken, Sr., and his sons, Bob and Pete. Knowles and Hyde formed a Knowles-Crapo Trust by pooling all the corporation's stock not owned by the three Millikens and actually held a majority of stock (689 of 1,144 shares)—but since each director cast one vote without regard to the shares he represented, the Millikens controlled. Thus Knowles and Hyde were outvoted on every issue of importance, by a count of three to two. "A very disagreeable business," Eliot Knowles remembered, a time of contention during which the opposing sides disagreed on virtually everything, "including the secretary's report."

The controversy came to an end in July, 1949, when the Millikens purchased the Knowles, Crapo and Tiffany stock at the price of $3,250 per share, for a total of more than $2,000,000. The Millikens financed the purchase through the sale of some of the company's liquid assets, chiefly securities, and paid the balance with the aid of bank loans. For the first time, the Milliken family was in absolute control of Mount Hope. J.K. held actual control through the Milliken Trust, but Bob and Pete had minor interests and were expected to inherit all of their father's holdings. Otherwise, there were only such minor holders as Al Curt, with three shares, and Doris Booth, with one share.

Of the Knowles-Milliken parting Eliot Knowles said, "Self-preservation ruled in that fight. The Millikens were together and so were we. I suppose they must have felt we held them up, but we were looking out for our own interests." For the moment it appeared that Mount Hope had entered an era of peace and harmony. There was no hint that this family rift presaged even more drastic changes in the fortunes of the firm.

🐦 Meanwhile, there was promise that the Milliken managerial line would continue. In December, 1948, the bells of North Dighton's churches began ringing to announce the birth of John Knowles Milliken, the son of Bob and Jean Milliken. Young Jake, as he was to be called, represented the sixth generation in the line of business entrepreneurs stretching back to the era of Thomas Knowles the whaling chief, some 150 years before. Jake was to be the family's first male heir in forty years to live to maturity. The future head of the family enterprise arrived with the qualified approval of his two-year-old sister Joan, whose Christmas wishes had already been made known. She wanted, first, a bike and second, a baby brother. Bob's family was complete. He and his wife had completed their role in helping to raise Helen's children before starting a family of their own.

"The Communists would choke"

The Korean war, which erupted so suddenly in 1950, brought to Mount Hope a brief boom and then a slowdown in business more serious than any the company had known since the great depression. For the first time in almost fifteen years, management was haunted by the prospect of short time and layoffs.

The Millikens were visited by Russell A. McCoy, Jr., of Columbia, South Carolina, a personable young engineer-salesman who represented Daniel Construction Company and was now seeking to persuade New England industrialists to move into the Carolinas. McCoy presented information on a number of promising sites for a new Mount Hope finishing plant, so effectively that the three Millikens and Frank Daylor went to North Carolina during the winter of 1950–51. J.K., the rugged individualist of Yankee tradition, met with North Carolina Governor Kerr Scott, a farmer-politician of equally independent spirit. The two strong-willed men liked each other at once. Scott sent the Millikens to experts in the Department of Conservation and Development, who guided them to available sites in Raleigh, Albemarle and Greensboro, as well as one in Butner, North Carolina, where a new state mental hospital was being created on a portion of a vast wartime army camp.

Butner had become familiar to many thousands of American troops during the war, including the celebrated Lightning Division; after the war other thousands had passed through for separation and return to civilian life—including the justly feared Rangers, the U.S. special forces of World War II.

Butner, however, wore a forlorn look that impressed neither Pete nor Bob Milliken, but it offered basic advantages: a site near the heart of the textile industry; an abundant water supply under state

Aerial view of Mount Hope Finishing Company, North Dighton, Massachusetts.

control; and an assemblage of motor pool shops built upon unusually thick concrete floors, ideal for the support of plant machinery.

The Millikens reached no decision during the winter, but they met with Charles Allen of Durham, a member of the State Board of Conservation and Development, and with John Umstead of Chapel Hill, an energetic and persuasive legislator who had already become the godfather of a new state mental hospital in Butner. Umstead had visions of an expansive industrial park amid the thousands of acres of pinelands surrounding the new institution. Umstead and Bob Milliken became fast friends and companions on numerous goose-hunting expeditions in eastern North Carolina. The relationship was to influence Mount Hope's future.

Further impetus to a southward move came from Frank Daylor, who continued to urge the creation of a new plant in close proximity to the textile industry that Mount Hope must serve in order to prosper. This proposal was carried to the point of completing a sketch and preliminary design for a Mount Hope branch plant, the work of John D. Latimer, a young architectural student at M.I.T. who had grown up in the Mount Hope "family."

Like many other sons of J.K.'s employees, John Latimer had gone to college with the aid of Mount Hope. The son of the plant's maintenance chief, John had worked at Mount Hope during the war as an engineer and had studied structural and civil engineering at a nearby college. After nine years as assistant plant engineer, John told Pete Milliken of his ambition to study architecture at M.I.T. Pete approved and kept John at 80 percent of his salary while he was a student. In exchange, Latimer helped at the plant whenever possible—and managed to complete his five-year course in three years.

Daylor, J.K and Bob Milliken were enthusiastic about Latimer's sketch of a branch plant and were strongly in favor of working toward a move southward. Pete Milliken was opposed to the idea. He felt that the destiny of Mount Hope, and his own as well, lay in North Dighton. These conflicting opinions may have aggravated the growing differences between Pete and Bob, differences which some observers felt had been influenced by Frank Daylor. The southern travelers, in any case, returned to Massachusetts in the late winter, to prepare for the celebration of Mount Hope's fiftieth anniversary.

Assistant Superintendent Albert Carr, who had run the plant in Pete's absence in the south, later recalled the dilemma to which the Millikens returned: "Times had really become bad. The Korean War boom ended overnight and a bust followed. The plant was already losing money. The reserve that we had set aside for payment of workers' bonuses was gone. Employees were grumbling, and competition from southern finishers was fierce.

"We were forced to put in short work-weeks, and did the best we could to maintain morale in the plant. Everyone in management saw that we should be cutting back harder, immediately, but we were in a pickle. Here we were on the verge of a big party celebrating our anniversary, with many of the leading people in the industry invited—and we just couldn't lay off hundreds of people at that moment, and cut back on all our benefits. As a matter of public relations it just couldn't be done. Those decisions had to be postponed, no matter what. And so they were."

In fact, 1951 was to be the first unprofitable year for the firm since the first year or so of its life. In January the plant was running 2,000,000 yards a week (50 percent below capacity); by Memorial Day it was down to 450,000 yards per week. The year's loss represented a steep decline from 1950, when the company had reported a net of some $250,000 on receipts of more than $4,500,000. By mid-summer J.K. and his sons agreed with Daylor that the trend must be reversed at all costs.

On the eve of the anniversary, reporter John Ackerman of the New Bedford *Standard-Times* visited North Dighton to survey Mount Hope at the age of fifty. He found it "a highly personal company" whose ways were unique:

"The Communists would choke on their pet hates at Mount Hope. They mutter in their beards darkly about oppressed workers under tyrannical capitalistic overseers, and they'd be lost if they got to North Dighton. What would the Communists make of a plant superintendent who gets mad when his workers call him Mister instead of Pete? What would they do with a man who has to retire at 65 after 40 years' work and angrily resents the fact that he has to stop working?

"What can you say of a factory executive who cheerfully insults the men under him with outrageous wisecracks and is promptly and cheerfully insulted in return with wisecracks even more outrageous if possible—or the man who, asked if Mount Hope was a good outfit to work for said simply, 'I've been there 30 years.' "

Ackerman discovered that though this busy concern was still finishing cloth at the rate of 100 million yards per year, it was operating in the absence of the conventional channels of management—literally without red tape. Workers who had a grievance went directly into Pete's office and sounded off, as they had to his father before him. Ackerman reported, "They are heard and heard with courtesy and the complaint acted on." To further this open-door policy the company had done away with private offices, though Pete had compromised in a few cases to build glass-walled cubicles opening into the general office space. Pete, so the reporter learned, had been forced into a private office by his men over his protest, and even so they had been forced to wait until Pete was out of town. They built his office and confronted him with a fait accompli upon his return. Pete had accepted the tribute grudgingly.

Ackerman noted that J.K. and his sons all lived so near the plant that any break in the smooth rhythm of the machinery usually was enough to send them running, day or night, to the plant, where they would arrive in a dead heat.

"An unusual company? Yes, especially in these days of huge, impersonal corporations. Behind the 50-year history of Mount Hope lies a sense of personal responsibility for the welfare of the workers on the part of management. Behind the success of the company lies a devotion to duty and a faith in hard work that is emblematic of all New England ever stood for."

Ackerman concluded that Mount Hope was "a triumph in the field of human relations," in stark contrast to the pattern in most American industrial firms. "Behind that triumph, however, is a sense of obligation. . . . That sense of personal responsibility was built into the plant from the start." The reporter cited the recent case of a worker who had gone to Pete Milliken to explain that he had gotten into debt so deeply that he owed more than $1,000 and

New York customers arrive by specially chartered train for Mount Hope's fiftieth-anniversary celebration.

that his creditors were hounding him. Pete worked out a plan under which Mount Hope paid the debts and the worker was to repay the company, without added interest, over a long period. When Pete asked how much should be deducted each week, the worker suggested $10. "That's too much," Pete said. He reduced the weekly payments.

Ackerman noted that the plant was not unionized and quoted Pete Milliken, "I think our people have sufficient confidence they'll receive fair treatment here without a union. Our wage scales and working conditions are right up there with union demands anywhere."

Fiftieth-anniversary clam bake.

By this time plans for a fiftieth-anniversary celebration were well under way. At the suggestion of Bob Milliken, and with the enthusiastic support of Harry Corr and other salesmen, Mount Hope was preparing to entertain. The party was conceived as a tribute to J.K. as founder and long-time chief executive, but its underlying purpose was to attract the attention of the textile industry to Mount Hope's specialized resources, in the hope of reversing the steady decline in volume of business. J.K. and Pete agreed, and a substantial investment was made to insure the success of the affair.

Under the urging of Harry Corr and the New York sales office, the company invited many of the key figures of the industry who were based in New York, not only customers but also mill executives, converters, stylists, designers, cloth brokers and selling agents. The converters invited, so Corr estimated, were responsible for selling "half the cloth sold in the U.S." Officers of Massachusetts textile plants were also invited. A number of insurance executives were to attend, most of them old friends acquired by J.K. during his almost forty years as director of Massachusetts Mutual Life.

The textile industry had never known such an event. A special train left New York the evening before the party, fourteen Pullman cars and two diners provided for Mount Hope's guests on the overnight trip to North Dighton. Ruth Donnegan of the New York staff remembered the run as almost interminable. "One other girl and I were hospitality hostesses for that crowd and I was up almost all night, walking back and forth through the cars, seeing that all of them had sandwiches, liquor and anything else they needed. It was my first trip on a Pullman and I was none too familiar with things, to say the least. The other girl became ill and went to bed and I had to carry on all alone. They kept me busy, since some of them were up all night. I was exhausted when the train pulled into the plant siding at about 6 A.M."

After breakfast aboard the train the New York guests were greeted by the Millikens and their wives, who stood in a receiving line beneath a bower of flowers and ferns. There was then a two-and-a-half-hour tour of the plant, which was running at full speed for the occasion. Guides conducted the visitors, explaining each step in the process as cloth passed from the grey room to the finished product. Guests were impressed by the three hundred-foot bleaching range, which was operated at a surprising rate of speed, and guides emphasized labor-saving devices in the plant, including a three thousand-foot conveyor system which eliminated traffic problems in warehousing and saved forty-eight hours in delivery of cloth, in addition to reducing the number of heavy trucks in use and virtually eliminating floor repairs. There was also a monorail elevator which carried finished goods to inspection and packing areas. Also on display was a fleet of fifteen-ton trailer trucks used for deliveries within a seventy-mile radius, the pride of Dighton Transfer, a Mount Hope subsidiary.

Visitors seemed to be astounded by the scale and capacity of the plant: twenty-seven acres of floor space, some 1,250,000 square feet, one of the largest finishing plants in the U.S., with a capacity of about four million yards of goods per week. The electric plant furnished 2,100 kilowatts per hour and was powered by nine boilers, which used fuel oil from storage reservoirs of 4,500,000 gallons. The plant consumed 10,000,000 gallons of water daily, drawn from the company's deep wells and the adjacent Three Mile River. Guides explained that much of the machinery and equipment had been designed and built by Mount Hope employees.

Guests paused for coffee and pastry in the cafeteria, which the company operated at a loss as an investment in worker morale. There was also an inspection of the extensive central records system, where some thirteen thousand spare parts were cataloged and all employee records were on file. The predominant impression as guests left the plant was of the remarkable cleanliness of the place—an impression made possible by the year-round attention of a one hundred-man maintenance force.

After the tour, the seven hundred out-of-town guests emerged into the park before the plant, where they were joined by about nine hundred Mount Hope employees amid the tantalizing aromas of a gigantic clam and lobster bake. The crowd gathered around five refreshment stands for an hour or more, then sat at long tables beneath the trees and began the consumption of fifty bushels of Essex clams and 1,500 lobsters. The Mount Hope glee club sang occasionally as the feast proceeded.

A few brief speeches brought the party to an end. Bob Milliken welcomed the guests and presented a silver bowl to Harry Corr for his work in "coordinating the needs of customers" with Mount Hope's production capacities. Pete Milliken added his greetings as

Fiftieth anniversary. Congressman Joe Martin (left) and J.K. Milliken, Sr. (Photo by Kennedy-Blake.)

plant superintendent and Bob introduced Joe Martin, who served as toastmaster. Martin praised J.K. for his "foresight, vision and humanitarianism" during Mount Hope's half century and as "a great builder for New England and America." Martin presented J.K. with a scroll signed by 150 of his close friends, and the congressman was presented in turn with a large portrait of his friend, General Douglas MacArthur.

Bernard Semel of New York, a converter who had been a customer of Mount Hope since 1901, gave a touching summary of his friendship with J.K. over the years and brought the crowd to its

Harry Corr (left) receives Salesmanship Award from Bob Milliken.

feet, cheering with his words of praise for the elder Milliken and his sons. J.K. stared down solemnly, blinking at the crowd.

Albert Carr and Al Curt were introduced as directors, a succession of speakers added their tributes to J.K., and Tim Manning, who had aided Mount Hope in the strike threat of 1934, presented J.K. with an engraved plaque as a memento of the occasion. There were others: William T. Read of New Bedford, a former president of the Morse Twist Drill Company, which J.K. had served as a director; L.J. Kalmbach, president of Massachusetts Mutual Life, of which J.K. was the oldest director; and William Nye, who had served with Milliken as director of the MassMutual board.

Also among the guests was Russell McCoy, the Carolina industrial-site evangelist who had so strongly impressed J.K. and Bob Milliken. The southerner was still pressing his case for a Mount Hope move to North Carolina.

Charles R. Briggs, one of Mount Hope's senior employees, presented J.K. with a massive silver service in behalf of the plant's workers, and J.K., still blinking rapidly, said hastily, "Thank you and all your faithful friends who have done so much for me over the years. . . . Thank you all for this wonderful day—it is a day I will never forget."

The New York guests passed through the plant once more, amidst the tinkling of fiftieth-anniversary chimes still resounding through the public address system, and boarded their train, only a few minutes late for their return trip.

All seemed to be well with Mount Hope. There was no hint of the troubles to come. The Milliken family, though fully aware of the seriousness of the problems posed by declining business, had no premonition of the impending disaster. They could not conceive of a crisis that would divide the family and bring about a strike of employees whose loyalty and friendship stretched back over two generations.

"To hell with the Millikens"

The strike came with a suddenness that shocked J.K. and his family. They had realized even during the fiftieth-anniversary celebration that employees were growing uneasy as business worsened and working hours were shortened. But though the work week dropped to four days, and then to three during July, no one in management conceived of the possibility of a strike.

It came on the heels of a reduction in company personnel. Toward the end of July, 1951, when it was clear that further retrenchments must be made, Pete held a discussion with Albert Carr and department heads, considering a list of employees to be laid off on the basis of seniority. On July 23 Pete and his staff concluded that they should reduce the work force by 20 percent—or 120 employees.

This word evidently spread through the plant. On the following day several workmen obtained union cards from the Textile Workers Union of America and began a drive for membership in the plant. They were remarkably successful. On July 27, the TWUA mailed Mount Hope a notice that 324 of 615 employees wished to join the union. Upon receiving the letter the next day, Pete Milliken consulted his father and brother and plant supervisors and announced that an additional sixty-five employees were being laid off. Two days later, before the company could reply to the union's notice, it was informed by the Boston office of the National Labor Relations Board that the TWUA had asked for certification—and had charged Mount Hope with failure to respond to notice of a union majority in the plant. It was clear that the union had notified the labor board and the company simultaneously, or almost so.

The Millikens declined to give automatic approval to an election.

They retained a new attorney, Edmund J. Blake of Boston, who had formerly represented the NLRB, and on his advice requested the board itself to conduct an election. This, Blake explained, was the company's right. If it agreed to a more informal "consent" election, some controversial issues, such as eligibility of certain employees to vote, would not be settled. J.K. accepted this advice with enthusiasm. He was particularly insistent that his workers have the right of a secret ballot.

Company lawyers met with William Sheehan, the NLRB field representative who had been hurried to North Dighton, but they declined to confer with Edward Doolan of the union until the NLRB had taken some action. Doolan waited in a separate room while Mount Hope lawyers consulted with Sheehan but soon departed for a union meeting at the South End Portuguese Club, where he assailed Mount Hope's refusal to recognize the TWUA and pictured "the stubborn Millikens" in terms that excited workers to indignation. The group voted to strike.

The sole issues of this extraordinary strike had been sounded: the refusal of the Millikens to recognize the union on its own terms; their speed-up in layoffs in the face of plant organization—and, perhaps most important of all, the dominant role of J.K. Milliken in village life. What had been accepted as open-handed philanthropy for two generations was viewed by the strikers as degrading paternalism.

The absence of traditional issues over which labor and management so frequently clashed drew widespread attention to this strike. From start to finish, no working conditions were to be argued, and neither wages nor hours were discussed by the contending parties. Except for heated exchanges over Mount Hope's motives in making a second round of layoffs, none of the usual controversies were to arise.

The first picket line appeared on August 13, at first a quiet, orderly group that included some veteran employees but was composed largely of younger men and women. J.K. looked down upon them from his second-floor office, his face reddening with anger when he saw near the head of the line the woman whose "blue baby" Jean Milliken had rushed to Boston scarcely a month earlier and whose stay at Children's Hospital had been paid for by Mount Hope. "If that's the way they feel," J.K. said, "it's all over. We might as well close the plant." He turned away as if he could no longer bear the sight of the woman and her husband in the picket line.

Jean and Irene Milliken shared J.K.'s indignation when they saw this woman in the picket line, accompanied by others for whom both women had done so much. One man who drew Jean's scornful attention was a former prisoner of war to whom she had sent help during her days as a volunteer Red Cross worker.

J.K. was feeling the strain of a serious family rift in these days as he and his sons and advisors anxiously debated the Mount Hope dilemma. Lines had already been drawn. Bob Milliken insisted on resistance to the end and a prompt move to the south, if necessary. His brother Pete insisted with equal firmness that they try to make peace with the union and continue operations in North Dighton, or, as a last resort, close the plant and leave the business.

During these days of stress, when it appeared that the workers were determined to organize Mount Hope or ruin it, the three strong-willed Millikens found themselves on a collision course. One afternoon J.K. emerged from a talk with Pete with tears in his eyes, and told Frank Daylor, Bob Milliken and the company's Taunton attorneys that he had asked Pete to leave for his waterfront home in Nonquitt, and to remain there until further notice. J.K. then turned to Bob, "Well, it's all your headache now. What are you going to do with it?" Bob said he would try to find new business for the plant and that Carr would take over day-to-day operations.

A day or so later Mount Hope made a rather cryptic announcement that Pete had been "relieved of all authority in respect to the company." Except for a brief mention in a speech by J.K. to employees a day or so later, Pete's departure was to have no further public mention. In later years Pete declined comment on the disagreement.

The strike had begun to divide other families in North Dighton. One of J.K.'s employees, James Smith, who had worked at Mount Hope for thirty-six years, was shocked when he heard that his son Raymond had passed around union cards. He told his son, "Okay, move with the boys if you want, but don't stick this out (pointing to his own neck). I still work there, you know."

Soon afterward, as he returned to work, Smith saw Raymond at the front of the picket line: "What is he but the leading lady in the parade? That's what nearly killed me. I gave him a blast that night, but it did no good."

The first week of the strike passed without further incident, and J.K. seemed hopeful that he might still reach some agreement with his workers. Through notices in the plant and newspapers he invited all production employees, strikers included, to his home on August 21 to hear his views on the dispute. The plant was closed for the occasion and office workers who were not involved in the strike were asked to remain at home.

A crowd gathered early to await J.K.'s appearance on the porch of his home, where a speaker's stand had been erected and a Taunton radio station's microphone was in place. The strikers arrived, some three hundred strong, led by Edward Doolan and accompanied by six town policemen. Marching two abreast they filed onto the circular driveway, carefully avoiding the freshly mown grass of the lawn. The day was hot and bright and men in shirtsleeves perspired as they waited. Half an hour passed. A couple of blue jays squawked and fluttered among the spruce and maple trees. J.K. and Bob Milliken came at last and, as the *Standard-Times* reporter noted, workers broke into applause. J.K. began to speak. He was one of the few men in the crowd who wore a coat and tie.

He read a speech that was obviously his own, speaking in a voice that was clear and steady but lacking its confidence of old. J.K. was barely a month past his seventy-sixth birthday, a vigorous, alert, rather plump figure. His white hair glistened in the sun, in striking contrast to the bushy black brows that dominated the craggy face. Milliken thanked his workers for coming out and said that for fifty years he had held open communication with all of those in the plant and that they had come to him with "suggestions, sometimes your criticisms, and occasionally your personal difficulties.

"Always you have been able to come to me with the assurance that I would listen, and that, whatever my decision, I felt you had confidence that it was based on . . . the best interests of all. It is in that spirit . . . that I talk to you today.

"The situation now confronting the Mount Hope Finishing Company is a trying one. I realize full well the effect it has on you, our families and this community. Likewise, it has had a very deleterious effect on me personally. North Dighton is my life. Here my roots are deeply established and here in North Dighton, God willing, I expect to die."

He spoke of growing southern competition in the textile industry and said that, though he might consider a southern plant in the future, he intended to operate in North Dighton "as long as we can operate efficiently and satisfactorily here." Milliken said he could think of no other way to explain his position to his old friends and employees: "Much as I would like to talk with each of you individually, it is simply not possible to do so." At that point, without preamble, as if the thought had been spontaneous, J.K. spoke of the harsh effects of the strike. "Already it has reached into my household in that the health of my son Pete has been seriously affected, so that he has been forced to take a long rest." He asked their cooperation in solving the company's problems and in regaining some of the customers who had already been lost during the strike.

"The time has arrived now, when we have got to decide whether we are going to be able to resume operations at this North Dighton plant." He reviewed the events leading to the strike, read the union's letter of notification that it had a majority of Mount Hope employees, and explained that he had been notified by the NLRB

almost immediately, charging the company with failure to respond
to union notice. "Obviously," J.K. said, "we had no opportunity to
reply, as the Union filed its petition the same day I received the
letter and before a reply could be made."

J.K. then reviewed the steps taken during meetings with the
union, the discussions of the eligibility of the employees who had
been laid off, and other matters. "Many of you employees may have
received the impression that the company is opposed to any election and will not allow an election to be conducted. This is not true.
The company is not opposed to an election to be conducted by the
National Labor Relations Board in which the employees can freely
and secretly vote as to whether they want the union to represent
them. . . .

"I founded this company fifty years ago. With the cooperation
and help of its many loyal employees over half a century we have
prospered and grown to our present size and position in the industry. Over this period . . . we have provided employment for many
people. We now have sons and grandsons of our early employees
working in the plant. During this time we have always tried to pay
fair wages, at least comparable to any of our competitors in this
area, and I believe that our working conditions and interest in the
welfare of our employees and their families have not been surpassed by any company in the industry.

"All of this has been accomplished without a union and I do not
believe that a union is necessary now. However, that is a matter for
you employees to decide for yourselves. You are free to vote and
decide whatever you feel to be in your best interest. . . . In my
opinion you employees have been ill-advised in taking this strike
action, which has done irreparable damage to you and your company in the loss of customers, business, and wages."

J.K. added that he would accept applications for work from all
employees, including those laid off: "If a sufficient number indi-
cate a desire to return to work, we will resume operations. We

would like to see the plant continue to operate and if you employees also wish to have it continue, we will cooperate with you."

He ended matter-of-factly but with the courtly air of an old man recalling the deserted North Dighton of 1901: "Now, ladies and gentlemen, as you know, I am not as young as I used to be. I would not be here today except that I feel I owe you a personal explanation of the situation as I see it. I would like you to think over what I have told you, discuss it . . . and act in accordance with what you think is for your own best interests.

"I wish to thank you all for coming here today and for your kindness in listening to me.

"I bid you good day."

Milliken disappeared into his house, the crowd dispersed, and calm settled over the village.

Later that evening the troubled worker James Smith urged his son Raymond to return to work. Raymond refused.

"Why not? You heard what the man said. Come back to work and they'll put as many in jobs as there is work to do. You heard him say it."

"You got the wrong interpretation," Raymond said.

"I can hear, can't I?" Smith shouted, but he saw that his effort was hopeless. "He was deaf to me. It's all a great shock. I'll never get over seeing him the leader in the parade." Like other older employees, Smith could not understand how workers could turn against J.K., whom they remembered fondly from numerous chance encounters at company picnics or outings, baseball games, on the street or in the plant, always hailed with a smile and a familiar J.K. greeting: "I don't know what I'd do without you, Jim," or, "You'll be here as long as I am." Jim Smith, as one news reporter divined, was finding it difficult to adjust to the coming of a new day.

The plant reopened on August 23. The strikers remained out, but the company announced that about 280 people were at work, among them some older men called back from retirement and a few married women whose employment had previously been banned. But a writer from the Taunton *Gazette* who toured the plant with Albert Carr reported that he had seen fewer than one hundred production workers—and that no more than thirty of those were tending machines. Carr was outraged by what he considered a distorted story and was fearful of its effect upon employees. J.K. Milliken announced his gratification at the display of loyalty that kept the plant running and said salesmen would redouble efforts to "keep those people employed." Still, attendance at the plant began to decline the day after the *Gazette*'s critical story appeared.

The NLRB held a brief session in Boston and ordered an election at Mount Hope to determine whether the union should bargain for the workers.

During the day pickets halted a freight train entering the Mount Hope siding to pick up goods. The trainmen, who were members of the Brotherhood of Railroad Trainmen, talked to the pickets, eyed a number of women who had driven up with bags filled with stones, and backed out of the siding, refusing to cross the picket lines. Truckers also turned back when threatened by strikers.

The Massachusetts Board of Arbitration and Conciliation entered the case, and the company and the strikers began negotiations in Boston, without making noticeable progress.

Back in North Dighton, the picket line became increasingly more rowdy. On August 30, little more than a week after J.K.'s appeal, the first violence erupted at the plant. Workers' automobiles were stoned and kicked and scratched with can openers. Eggs and tomatoes were hurled at car windows; the tomatoes, so salesman Harry Corr noted, were armed with razor blades and bits of glass, "and mothers and kids were throwing them, too." A jar of yellow paint was hurled through a car's windshield, sugar was poured into gas tanks, and nails were strewn across the streets. Strikers smashed a few windows in the plant by hurling stones, one of which narrowly missed striking Bob Milliken while he was in the calender room. Several stones were found on the plant floor, and production declined among the skeleton work force, which was now composed largely of women.

Shouts and curses rose from the picket line when workers came or went—but salesman Corr's passage was an exception. He spent his time during the strike traveling to and from textile mills in the region, bringing in orders and samples in an effort to keep the plant in operation. When he first approached the line and was shoved back by imported union men, Corr's neighbors protested. "Let him through, he's trying to keep it open for you. He's selling orders." Corr was not molested thereafter.

Felix Buba, a World War II navy pilot who had worked in the plant for about a year, found crossing the picket line an unsettling experience: "It was a frightening thing to be cooped inside a car with several other workers, creeping along while that mob of angry, red-faced, bitter men and women shouted obscenities and shook fists and clubs at you, just a few inches outside the window—and these were people I had known as friends and fellow workers."

Buba found the ordeal of leaving the plant hardly less trying: "We drove our cars the length of the plant as fast as we could go in there—up to 15 miles an hour, I suppose—trying to avoid the pickets. We would spot them at one gate, then zip down to the other one, flying past the ranges, and get out before the strikers could catch us."

Such escapes were managed despite bicycle brigades of youngsters who aided the pickets, serving as lookouts and messengers and bringing them supplies. By now, as one newspaper reported, North Dighton's telephones "hummed with threats" as tension rose between strikers and loyal workers. Anonymous callers threatened the homes of workers.

On September 10, the week after the first outbreak of rowdiness and threats, Mount Hope sought a temporary injunction against the union, before Judge H.T. Cahill in Boston. The company said it feared for life and property in the village. These fears were confirmed on September 11, while the case was still under consideration.

During the morning, parading strikers punctuated their catcalls with chants of "Tonight's the night!" Many workers went to the South End Portuguese Club during the evening to drink beer. Several families of the plant's loyal workers received threatening telephone calls throughout the day, warning housewives that they should persuade their husbands to join the union for their safety.

A mob of four hundred to five hundred men and women gathered in Summer Street after nightfall, a few blocks from J.K.'s house, and began hooting at loyal employees, several of whom sat on their front porches waiting, with shotguns across their knees. The mob ran along the street, and there were sounds of stones crashing into the house, shattering windows. A chorus of shouts and screams filled the night.

James McGowan, a Mount Hope receiving foreman who was a much-decorated Marine veteran of World War II, was on his porch when the barrage struck: "Two of the rocks, as big as pineapples, smashed through the screened porch door, and carried through two windows. My baby was sleeping not six feet away from where a huge boulder came through the window."

McGowan and his wife carried the baby and their four-year-old daughter into a hallway and closed doors to protect them. McGowan snatched his .38 revolver and ran outside, where he found his next door neighbor, Spud O'Connell, the plant transportation manager, who had also come under attack.

When the stones struck the O'Connell house, Mrs. O'Connell went into the yard, turned on the garden hose, and began sprinkling the mob. A man ran through the gate and struck her savagely beneath one eye. O'Connell clubbed the assailant with his shotgun and then, joined by his teenaged sons and McGowan, began showering the crowd with apples gathered from his lawn. When this had no effect O'Connell and McGowan fired one or two shots each into the air. As McGowan remembered it, "The neighbors came to help us and they brought guns with them; it was just like Minute Men.

There was about 15 or 20 of us against this mob. They ran like rats
when they heard the guns go off."

O'Connell and McGowan charged toward parked cars which had
driven up with the mob, and the drivers moved away. The street
was cleared for a time, but some of the mob straggled back, and it
was 1:30 A.M. before quiet returned to the neighborhood. Several
men sat up all night, waiting with their guns.

Mount Hope, now thoroughly alarmed, sought protection from
state and county officials. Police Chief John Synan asked for two
deputies from New Bedford but got no response from the sheriff
there. Synan telegraphed Governor Dever in Boston, reporting the
mob action, the use of firearms, and a situation "now out of
control"—and requested state police or National Guard protection
for North Dighton. The governor's office declined to intervene
until assured that "local resources had failed" to control violence,
"and that means real violence, not just a few rocks thrown and a
woman squirting a hose and somebody slapping her for it."

Area newspapers denounced the refusal of Dever to send aid to
North Dighton. The New Bedford *Standard-Times* accused the governor of resorting to "legal platitudes" and of "either an abject
failure to meet the responsibility or an almost incredible inability to
evaluate a very bad situation." The Providence *Journal* saw the
Dighton violence as "an ugly forewarning of trouble," and added,
"We hope that the people and press of Massachusetts compel Dever
to take his head out of the political sand and give the law-abiding
citizens of Dighton the support they want and need."

Westbrook Pegler, the columnist who often assailed unions for
abuse of power, called the Mount Hope incident "another flagrant
case of mob terrorism by criminal unioneers," and declared that
the besieged householders "would have been within their rights
had they blown the heads off as many of the terrorists as they could
hit with their shotguns"—and cited a recent case in support of his
opinion.

Representative Francis Harding of Dedham declared, "When a man has to get a gun out and shoot to protect his wife and his home, it is far more than a labor dispute." Harding joined other state House Republicans in calling for an investigation of Dever's failure to send police to North Dighton.

Most regional newspapers tended to view the impasse between the Democratic governor and the staunchly Republican Millikens in terms of partisan politics—and political ties may have led Edward Doolan to the one journal that proved friendly to the union cause.

The Boston *Pilot,* an organ of the Archdiocese of Boston, gave prominent display to Doolan's attack on the reign of J.K. Milliken: "Recent events in Dighton read like a page out of the nineteenth century. . . . A 'company town' may be very quiet and picturesque, especially tucked away in the rolling hills of Massachusetts, but it manages to contain at the same time some dreadful restrictions on the human freedom of its people brought about by the excessive liberties of a few. It is understandable that 'the few' involved are reluctant to see such a world disappear, BUT FOR THE SAKE OF THE GENERAL WELFARE, GO IT MUST."

Doolan also charged that the coming of the union to Dighton had been the "inevitable outgrowth of a long persecution" by the Millikens, who had been "ruggedly immune to normal emotions, aspirations and ideals that motivate human beings."

"This is not the case," the *Standard-Times* retorted. "At Mount Hope the management in a documented record of 50 years proved a genuine and warm interest in its employees by providing superior wages, working facilities and personal contact that for years was unequalled in the industry. There was economic protection in good times and bad. If there were 'dreadful restrictions' they were not readily apparent to the employees until the summer of 1951—a half century after the founding. At this date there is still no union or personnel complaint on any conditions for workers at Mount Hope.

"Perhaps this unusual relationship had to go under changing

standards of what constitutes 'freedom,' but there was also no excuse for what occurred. . . . It may be important to the public welfare to resist such a high-handed, completely unjustified attitude as has been shown by the union and the State to a long-established member of the community."

In mid-September the North Dighton Board of Selectmen fired its chairman, William Hathaway, an accountant for Mount Hope, as well as Police Chief John Synan, who had been chief for thirty-two years and was also traffic manager at Mount Hope, as well as the town's fire chief and a deputy sheriff. These dismissals were for the duration of the strike, to avoid conflicts of interest.

The Selectmen named Wilbur Menges, a lanky former army captain, acting head of the police force. Menges lost no time in lecturing the pickets, demanding an end to violence. He assured them of their right to peaceful picketing but warned that the police would keep peace at all costs. "There will be no need for guns," Menges said. "I'm calling in all firearms right now." But though he threatened a house-to-house search for firearms, Menges did not carry it out.

Edward Doolan closed a union meeting on the night of September 12 by urging members to get out the vote for the certification election, "but no rough stuff. Get to bed early. The town's swarming with out of town reporters and they'll be watching you." Later, Doolan told reporters that the riot of the previous evening had been merely "propaganda on the part of management, because they know they've lost the strike."

J.K. Milliken was one who agreed with Doolan's prediction. He stopped in Albert Carr's office during the day and asked, "How are you getting along with these people in negotiations?"

Carr thought Milliken might suspect that he favored the union cause. "Well, I treat them decently," Carr said. "I call them by their first names, but I'm just polite. No further contacts, if that's what you mean."

"Well, I'll tell you," J.K. said. "We're going to lose this election."

"I don't believe it."

"We are. We'll have a union. And we'll make more money than before. These employees will be dependent on the union for everything, and not on Mount Hope. And don't forget that you're the man who will have to deal with their stewards every day. I don't want you to get into such animosity in your relationships that you can't deal with them."

Events then moved rapidly toward a climax. Workers voted overwhelmingly in favor of the union, by 369 to 210. The company and TWUA representatives met in Boston the following day and came to an agreement: the mill would reopen, and all employees, including the 190 who had been laid off, would be rehired within a month—with the proviso that work time must be shared; if business remained bad there would be short work weeks.

J.K.'s optimism returned. The next morning he addressed workers in the plant over the loudspeaker system: "The strike is over. A settlement has been reached. I am happy to report that the strike is over." There was a celebration in the plant, but it was short-lived indeed. The new union local's membership rejected the contract; it now insisted that Mount Hope take back all workers, immediately.

J.K. called an emergency session of directors. Al Curt came up from New York and met the others at Bob Milliken's house. It was obvious that the union's defiance had made the division among the Milliken family even more pronounced. Bob sided with his father against Pete, supporting a last-ditch fight against the union and a southward move. Pete, who was present, had nothing to say during the meeting. Discussion was brief.

J.K. was firm in his announcement that he would close the plant: "What decided me was the halting of our shipping of goods. We were caught with more than 10,000 packages of finished goods that belong to our customers, not to mention 3500 bales of grey goods and others in process. The value of goods is from $3,000,000 to $5,000,000. I won't risk a second experience like this—we can't do it."

He also spoke of a move to the south: "When we located here, we were in the heart of the textile industry, but since it's all gone south, we've been fading away. A finishing plant is only a glorified laundry, and we must be near the origin of the wash."

J.K. added that he had given in to many union demands, but the final one—that he return all hands to work the next day—was the last straw. Every employee realized that it would take ten days to prepare the plant for opening since there were no goods ready for processing. The decision of the directors was all but unanimous. Pete Milliken voted, "Present." The meeting broke up with the understanding that the plant would close immediately, and except for Bob's needs in the south, all machinery and equipment would be sold; the real estate was to be put on the market at once. Bob and Frank Daylor would carry out their plan to open a smaller plant in the south.

Reporters who found Bob Milliken late in the day gathered from him some unguarded comments that would be remembered. Herman Mello of the Fall River *Herald-News* quoted Bob as saying that the plant would be closed "permanently" within a month, that management was "fed up with unabated threats and economic and financial pressure exerted by the union, and just can't take it any longer." The tentative plan to move to the south had now become an immediate order of business.

The strikers scoffed as this newspaper story was passed around town: "They're bluffing. Millikens would never leave Dighton. They're trying to trick us."

Even the posing of the threat of the move south made thoughtful people in Dighton apprehensive for the future. The loss of Mount Hope would be a disaster of major proportions. Not only was the plant the only local employer of importance; it bore more than a third of the tax burden and over the years, as the result of J.K.'s informal assumption of responsibilities, had undertaken more of the costs of public services than people realized. The town faced the loss of the hospital and inexpensive medical care, free maintenance of homes and yards, free or low-cost upkeep of streets and

roads, cheap power and coal, milk and eggs. The community mus
undergo a complete revision of its ways of life.

One local leader declared that the town had an opportunity for
improvement in the situation. The Reverend James K. Allen of the
local Unitarian Church proposed that local people band together
to buy the plant for a cooperative venture of some kind. "Dighton
has made one man so rich he does not have to care about anyone
else," Allen said. "I think local capital and labor may be able to
form another business enterprise to carry on in this splendid loca
tion." It was not to be.

In Boston, where company and union representatives met daily
under the guidance of state officials, the talks dragged on without
result. Once, when a TWUA official questioned the value of further talks he was assured by Edmund J. Blake, the new company
lawyer, that newspaper accounts of the closing were inaccurate and
that the plant would continue to operate if an agreement could be
reached. By this time, as Bob Milliken recalled it later, machinery
was already being shipped from the plant, bound for Butner,
North Carolina.

All grey goods received after September 19 were returned to
customers or sent elsewhere for finishing. Unfilled orders for supplies were cancelled.

Within a week major changes had been made in the firm's
financial affairs. Bob Milliken and Frank Daylor bought control of
the capital stock through transfers worked out by attorneys and J.K.
From J.K., who still acted as trustee, Bob and Daylor took an option
on the Milliken Foundation stock, whose purchase price was set at
$500,000. By October 5 the two had also taken an option on Pete's
stock, with a value of more than $300,000, and within three weeks
had completed that transaction. The final phase of these stock
exchanges was to be completed when the North Carolina enterprise had been launched. Meanwhile, Bob took an option on the
Butner property under a lease arrangement.

By October 20, when the Dighton plant closed for good, Bob's

North Carolina attorneys had formed the Creedmoor Corporation, under which the Butner plant was to be operated. Hand-picked employees from Mount Hope were on the way south.

Those who were familiar with the century-old history of the Knowles-Milliken enterprises must have been struck by the parallel between the closing of Mount Hope of Massachusetts and the breakup of Thomas Knowles and Company in the twilight of the whaling era. In each case changing times had brought upheavals, and in each case two brothers had left the firm to go their separate ways.

Stuart Robertson, whose Robertson Factories was to remain a major customer, viewed the southward move with misgivings: "I thought Bob was crazy to go down there. I asked him why he insisted, and he said that he felt he ought to keep the family name going. He was determined that the Milliken tradition would live on. So each brother went his own way. Pete stayed in Massachusetts. Bob took the risk and started afresh, but with much-reduced capital."

When it was all over, and it was clear that Mount Hope would never reopen in North Dighton, there was little agreement on the causes of the strike. Even those who had been closest to center of rapidly moving events differed widely on the factors which had caused the upheaval. Some felt that the presence of Daylor, as an outsider in the family firm, had been disrupting, causing dissension between Pete and Bob Milliken and contributing to labor unrest. Others insisted that the problem was merely economic, that declining business made layoffs inevitable and resistance by employees virtually automatic. The veteran English employee Johnny Brooks agreed with Al Curt that returning war veterans had brought on the strike since they had come back from global travels with new ideas of how they should be treated and paid for their work. The New Bedford *Standard-Times* detailed that theory:

"The union movement was led by younger workers. . . . There was a desire for excitement, for a power—through unionization—

that could distate to the Millikens. At a nearby club, the younger men, between beers, persuaded each other that they were chattels. . . ."

Johnny Brooks had a similar version of these troubles: "Some of the boys coming back from war were given jobs that dependable old-timers had been holding down—maybe they weren't well-educated, but they knew their jobs and the kids coming in green didn't know them. The upshot of it was that it didn't work. They had to take the veterans out of those jobs, and that's where the trouble began."

Albert Carr felt that the critical article in the Taunton *Gazette* had compounded Mount Hope's problems: "Plant attendance began to decline after that erroneous story appeared. People in the various departments knew that people were at work where they were—but they read the newspaper and thought that others were staying out, so more and more of them stayed away. That was the turning point. I'll always swear the *Gazette* ran Mount Hope out of North Dighton with that very hostile story. By the time out-of-town newspapers came in to print the truth, it was too late."

Neither Pete nor Bob Milliken agreed that returning war veterans or the newspaper had caused the strike. And Mrs. Bob Milliken said, "The strike was triggered by the rumor that Mount Hope was moving south."

Harry Corr had a further idea: "The fiftieth anniversary party brought it on—though there was already discontent. All the help went to the clambake, of course, and enjoyed the clams and lobsters and all the rest. But when it was over the union told them the company shouldn't have spent all that money for the party, but put it into pay envelopes instead."

Red Staples felt that the strike was brought on by "a few second-generation wise guys." Staples, who ran one-fourth of the plant under Pete Milliken's supervision, later remembered, "Hard times made it necessary to lay off people. We did as much of it as possible on the basis of seniority, but it couldn't all be that way, because some junior men ran key machines and had to be kept. That meant that

some fellows who'd been there 12 or 15 years had to be laid off.
They couldn't understand that. So they joined the strike, too."

Pete Milliken's view was that his father's physical and mental state
had an effect on the outcome. "Father wasn't himself by a long way
at that time. He was in no condition to face anything like that. His
health declined very rapidly after that time, too.".Others disagreed,
pointing out that J.K., Sr., remained active and mentally alert for
years, until the onset of his fatal illness.

In a summary of the strike and its aftermath, the New Bedford
Standard echoed J.K.'s thought that Mount Hope could have operated at lower cost with a union. "Paternalism was expensive. The
company rented houses to the employees at half the Federal ceiling
rate. A good bungalow with plenty of lawn rented for $4 a week for
years, rose to $6.50 during World War II and at closing was $8. A
comparable home in any other textile community would be at least
$15. The company mowed all grass for less than cost. It helped
support the North Dighton police. It provided funeral cars for
nothing. It paid generous pensions . . . and gave hospital care at a
loss. . . . This was non-union paternalism."

But that in itself was the hidden issue of the strike. Most employees instinctively yearned for greater independence and came to
resent the Milliken generosity. Many of them expressed this
subconsciously to reporters: "J.K. hates unions . . . he wouldn't let
us organize . . . those stubborn Millikens . . . to hell with the
Millikens."

Whatever the causes, the Massachusetts phase of Mount Hope
operations had ended. The future lay in the south.

The union was not the cause"

✦ The Textile Workers Union of America wasted no time in forcing the migrant company to trial. It filed a complaint against Mount Hope with the National Labor Relations Board in December, 1951, charging unfair labor practices. The board responded in May, 1952, with a formal complaint charging the company with several violations of the Taft-Hartley Act. Violations included the layoffs of 185 employees, closing of the North Dighton plant, and refusal to bargain.

As successor to the Massachusetts corporation, the struggling little firm of Mount Hope, North Carolina, was charged as accountable for these violations. The firm was ordered to pay back wages and moving expenses of employees—costs estimated at about $2,000,000. It was also ordered to rehire all Massachusetts workers who wished to move to North Carolina, even if it must dismiss all its employees to do so. But the complaint, by some oversight of counsel for the board, failed to state charges against Mount Hope, North Carolina, clearly and unequivocally. A memorable courtroom skirmish was to be fought over this issue.

A hearing before a trial examiner for the NLRB was set for June 16, in Taunton, Massachusetts, and the man chosen by the board was C.W. Whittemore, who was well-known for his sternness in dealing with management and for his dedication to the cause of labor. Whittemore, a veteran of the NLRB's early days, was a layman rather than a lawyer.

As one of the nation's first cases against a "runaway" corporation under the Taft-Hartley Act, the Mount Hope affair attracted unusual attention in legal circles. Though New England textile plants had been moving southward for years, and one or two had been prosecuted under the New Deal's old Wagner Act, this case was to be tried under the new, Republican-sponsored Taft-Hartley Act, which was presumably more favorable to management. Unfortunately for Mount Hope, however, the two acts had virtually the same provisions covering "runaway" corporations.

Mount Hope had been singled out as an apparently easy target. The board assigned the best of its personnel to the case, and both board and counsel were confident.

For their defense Bob Milliken and his father chose Walter Powers to represent Mount Hope, Massachusetts. They heeded the advice of Frank Fuller, their Durham, North Carolina, counsel and retained Thornton H. Brooks of Greensboro, North Carolina, as attorney for the North Carolina corporation. Brooks was already a veteran of fourteen years' labor practice, a tall, reserved man of deceptively mild manner who spoke in the soft accents of his native region. He was the son of Aubrey L. Brooks, a noted trial lawyer, author and historian. It was young Brooks who would direct the case, plot and conduct its strategy, and pursue it vigorously in face of formidable obstacles.

Brooks made his first move by mail, petitioning Whittemore to exclude the North Carolina corporation from the case. He also requested hearings in North Carolina, where company records could be produced with convenience. Whittemore refused to exclude the new corporation and reserved judgment on the North Carolina hearings. He also denied Brooks permission to appeal these rulings.

Though the Tar Heel lawyer was convinced that Mount Hope had violated no laws, he was not encouraged as he began preparing the case. Since a key question was whether the company had laid off employees because of union activities, Brooks realized that he must know what the attitude of Pete Milliken would be. After an unproductive interview with Pete, Brooks expected damaging testimony from him as a government witness. The union, on the other hand, hoped that Pete would concede that he had chosen union members for the layoffs—which would have been a flagrantly unfair labor practice.

When the hearing opened before a sizeable crowd in the Taunton courthouse, one of the most apprehensive observers was J.K. Milliken, Sr. He sat beside John Moorhead of Durham, North Carolina, his public relations counsel. Both men were dismayed by the hostile attitude of Whittemore as the hearing opened.

Before evidence had been taken, Whittemore assailed Brooks with the query: "Do you know of a case where it is possible for three individuals to incorporate themselves out of liability under the Federal act?" Having thus revealed his view of the case, the examiner overruled all of Brooks' objections to testimony dealing with Mount Hope, North Carolina.

Whittemore then rejected virtually all lines of evidence which Brooks sought to introduce, including testimony as to the early search for a Mount Hope plant site in North Carolina, southern leadership in modern textile manufacturing, and economic conditions that Mount Hope maintained had brought on the strike.

There were times during the tense Taunton hearing when Whittemore actually seemed to take over the direction of the board's case. From the start, Brooks protested that the complaint as drawn failed to allege any violation "upon which relief could be granted." Once Whittemore had grasped the implication of this protest, he literally forced the NLRB counsel to amend his complaint. An extended altercation ensued.

Brooks insisted: "The complaint says that the thing that North Carolina has done wrong, if any, is to be a successor corporation. . . . What violation of the National Labor Relations Act is it to be a successor corporation? . . . It is not a violation. . . ."

Whittemore turned to Sidney Coven, counsel for the board: ". . . I would like the assurance of Mr. Coven that he has no intention of claiming . . . that there have been any actual unfair labor practices taking place in the plant in North Carolina, that that is not an issue before me."

Coven: "No, except insofar as North Carolina is just a continuation of the business in Massachusetts, and continues the refusal to bargain."

"In other words," Whittemore said, "in . . . language which we all understand, you are simply claiming that this is a 'runaway shop'?"

"That's right, sir."

Brooks responded, "I'm not sure what you mean. . . . There is no allegation here that North Carolina was formed for the purpose of evading the Act."

Whittemore: ". . . I gathered from Mr. Coven's opening statement that he is claiming very definitely that the move . . . was to evade its responsibilities under the Act. . . ."

Brooks: "But he has not alleged that, and he is bound by his allegations, unless he asks to amend his complaint. . . ."

Whittemore then asked Coven if he agreed that Mount Hope was a "runaway shop." Coven agreed, and Whittemore said: "If that is your actual allegation, is there any reason why you don't allege it? . . . I think Mr. Brooks is justified in asking that he know . . . definitely what your contention is. . . . I can see now what he is getting at."

Coven said, "I fail to see why it is necessary to amend the complaint. . . . I don't see, frankly, how we can make any allegation in the complaint that North Carolina did commit a violation of the law prior to October 16 [1951, its date of incorporation]."

"That isn't the point," Whittemore said. "It would appear to me . . . that you should be able to compose a very brief paragraph to amend the complaint . . . and I think it would cover what Mr. Brooks has pointed out is at least a lack—although I am not saying that it is a fatal lack. . . . Well, just let me suggest that at the first recess you consider the matter."

Under this urgent prodding, Coven returned after a recess with a new paragraph as an amendment to his complaint:

"Respondents, Mount Hope, Massachusetts, Joseph K. Milliken,

Robert D. Milliken, and Frank L. Daylor did on or about September 19, 1951, discontinue their finishing operations in North Dighton, Massachusetts, and did, on or about October 16, 1951, organize . . . Mount Hope, North Carolina, all for the purpose of evading their responsibility and obligations under the Act to bargain collectively with the union."

Brooks objected, on the ground that the board had ample time to amend the complaint before the hearing. He also insisted that Whittemore allow the Millikens time to prepare a defense. He was overruled, and the amendment was accepted as part of the complaint.

At one point Coven asked Frank Daylor to explain his connection with Mount Hope, North Carolina, during the corporate transfer when officers and stockholders filled temporary roles.

"I believe I'm Vice President," Daylor said.

Whittemore broke in to cross-examine, "Well, you believe you are. Don't you know whether you are or not?"

"No, sir. I don't know."

"Why don't you know? Are your business interests so many you don't know whether you are a vice president of a certain company or not?"

"If I am Vice President, it is a purely nominal capacity. I have no particular duties there, or anything of that sort, but I understand I have been elected vice president."

Daylor was then asked to explain the status of machinery shipped from North Dighton to the Butner plant. "It's carried on an open account," he said, ". . . just an account of how much money they owe us."

Whittemore interrupted once more: "You mean the two Millikens haven't decided what they are going to pay the two Millikens?"

"No, I don't mean that at all, sir. I have a very vital interest in what's paid the Mount Hope Finishing Company of Massachusetts for machinery; and the agreement is that they will pay not less than the highest Office of Price Stabilization price for the machinery."

The board's counsel then resumed the examination of the witness.

The hearing became a series of objections by Brooks, virtually all of which were made in vain. While Bob Milliken was on the stand, Brooks asked what percentage of goods on hand had come from the Carolinas and Virginia and what percentage from other states. Whittemore sustained an objection to this question and suggested that Brooks make an offer of proof, to which Brooks replied, "If permitted to answer, the witness would answer that for a representative period in June, 1952, approximately 82 per cent of the goods in process derived from customers in North Carolina, South Carolina and Virginia, and approximately the remaining 18 per cent comes from other states."

Whittemore: "Very well, the offer may remain in the record. It is, however, rejected."

At another point Whittemore admitted in evidence an article in the Fall River *Herald News* quoting Bob Milliken as to his refusal to bargain with the union and his pronouncement that the North Dighton plant had been closed permanently and that operations would move south. The author of the article, Herman Mello, was allowed to testify over the objection of Brooks. But when the defense sought to introduce an article Mello had written only the previous day, clarifying Bob Milliken's connections with Mount Hope, North Carolina, Whittemore declined to admit it—and also declined to allow Mello to testify as to whether he had written the second article.

The controversy between Whittemore and Brooks over the admission of newspaper articles revealed the sharpness of their exchange. During the examination of the union organizer Harold Schofield, Brooks said, "I assume that . . . General Counsel is not, by the introduction of the newspaper, taking that as evidence of the facts, but merely of what the article says."

Whittemore: "It is received as a basis for any action which this witness may have taken as a result of having seen it; also, I will put you on notice that if there are any quotations in there from any of the individuals who are Respondents who responded and are not rebutted, then I shall take them for granted as being quoted."

Brooks: "If that's the case, [I] certainly should read it."

Whittemore: "I'm putting you on notice, Mr. Brooks—"

Brooks: "I didn't understand we could try things by newspaper . . . they are certainly hearsay evidence . . . the best evidence is the person who said them."

Whittemore overruled the objection and accepted the articles, "only for the purpose of showing what this witness—what action this witness may have taken as a result of seeing them," but then added, "not as to the truth of any statements made therein unless and until the one who may be quoted there is on the witness stand."

After an extended argument Brooks won a limited victory on a single point—Whittemore did not require Mount Hope, North Carolina, to show its records during the hearing and suggested to Coven that he move for a further hearing in North Carolina to put the records into evidence. Coven said he felt that Bob Milliken could offer all essential evidence.

The parade of witnesses was long, and most of them were put through extensive direct and cross-examination, with frequent legal skirmishing over admission of their testimony. In addition to Pete and Bob Milliken, Frank Daylor and Schofield, Whittemore heard from Edward F. Doolan of the union; Edmund Blake, the Mount Hope lawyer; David Grodsky, a conciliator with the Massachusetts Board of Arbitration and Conciliation; Herman Mello, the Fall River reporter; Albert Carr, assistant superintendent, and John S. Mather, purchasing agent, of the North Dighton plant; John Soares and Austin Sullivan, formerly of Massachusetts, who had been summoned from their new jobs at Butner; and Frederick V. Moulding, a former employee.

Moulding offered a bit of new evidence that was of especial interest to the Millikens when he revealed that it was he who had first approached the union about coming into the Mount Hope plant. Moulding was an Englishman of about fifty years of age, a World War I veteran.

But it was Pete Milliken who offered the evidence that was the highlight of the opening day. His father seemed to stiffen in his seat when Pete took the stand. John Moorhead noticed that when Pete was asked if their union views had anything to do with the selection of the employees to be laid off, J.K. Milliken grasped the arms of his chair so tightly that veins swelled forth in his white hands. Morehead recalled, "Pete had been subpoenaed by the union. If he wanted to sabotage his father and Bob, this was his opportunity. You could have heard a pin drop in the courtroom when he pondered the question and then said sharply, 'No! We had no idea who had signed union cards.' "

Pete was equally straightforward, if less helpful to management, on why he had laid off an additional sixty-five workers: "Business was worse than we could possibly have anticipated, and we could easily get along without that approximate 30 per cent . . . of the payroll, and we felt if by chance we might at some later date find it difficult to reduce the number on the payroll, it was serving the best interest of the company to make one move."

Pete's later testimony also caused Brooks some concern. "I was well aware," Pete said, "that in order to lay off, if you had a union shop, you would be required to negotiate and barter on the thing, and it seemed to me that it was so obvious that we were going to have to do it anyway, that we might just as well get it behind us." This statement was to be interpreted by the union and the board as a tacit admission that Mount Hope had stepped up its layoffs in order to hamper union activity.

At the end of the first day, J.K. Milliken, Sr., was so angered and frustrated by Whittemore's conduct of the hearing that he was almost physically ill, and he refused to attend other sessions. The hearing continued for four and a half days. At the end Whittemore said that the hearing was unexpectedly brief since both sides "hewed to the issues."

The Mount Hope officials had no cause for optimism when it was over, and Brooks returned to J.K.'s home in North Dighton that evening to warn his client that Whittemore was likely to find against them on every count. Brooks had planned an appeal to the federal courts from the start and had prepared for that by making about fifty exceptions during the hearing. His hope of overturning Whittemore's ruling lay in the examiner's bias and in his errors or faulty interpretations.

J.K. was impressed by the stout defense Brooks had made. He wrote a friend, "We could find no lawyer around here who would be any good. Bob sent a young man by the name of Brooks from Greensboro who seems to know what it is all about."

Whittemore's report appeared on August 15—a finding that Mount Hope had violated the law as charged. He concluded that Mount Hope was a "runaway" and that the new corporation should be held liable for all violations charged and must pay the penalties. These promised to be ruinous. Since there were 615 eligible employees on the payroll at the time of the strike, and the average wage in finishing plants, by federal figures, was $3,250 per year, it was calculated that aggregate back pay would amount to more than $2,000,000, to say nothing of some $250,000 to $300,000 in estimated moving costs for Massachusetts employees going to Butner. Even deducting other wages earned by employees in the interim, or wages lost in seasonal layoffs, Mount Hope faced disaster in case the verdict stood. There was also the prospect of increased awards of about $2,000,000 a year if the case dragged on. NLRB officials conceded that this would be a record award, far exceeding the $1,600,000 back-pay penalty against Republic Steel in 1940.

The next step in the case was a hearing before the full board of the NLRB in Washington, but Brooks regarded that as little more than a formality. He expected the board to approve the report of its examiner with little ado. Even so, he attacked aggressively, denouncing Whittemore's report as "more becoming a prosecutor's brief than the report of an 'unbiased and impartial' examiner" as envisioned by the law. The findings, Brooks said, "were not according to the facts," and he charged that Whittemore "acted as an interested party and assumed the role of prosecutor by advising, suggesting, and insisting, that General Counsel amend the complaint."

Once more Brooks sought to have the record reopened, so that more testimony could be taken as to the status of the North Carolina corporation. The NLRB refused him.

The Millikens had the feeling that they were lost in a New Deal house of mirrors, fated to wander through the case indefinitely, lost at every turn. But winds of political change were sweeping the country, and some of the Millikens took heart. Harry Truman was in the last days of his presidency, and Dwight Eisenhower was elected in November, 1952. But Brooks was looking to the federal courts rather than the White House. His goal was the U.S. Court of Appeals for the Fourth Circuit with jurisdiction over the Carolinas, Virginia, West Virginia and Maryland. Brooks was most familiar with the conservative views of that court. He realized that the board's lawyers would attempt to docket the case in the First District, in Massachusetts, whose court was likely to be more sympathetic to the union's cause. Since the first party to docket the appeal in a federal appellate court would determine the locale of the appeal hearing, Brooks anticipated a race for the courthouse. He was determined to win.

The Mount Hope case went before the National Labor Relations Board in Washington in April, 1953, when Brooks was joined as counsel by the Washington firm of Reilly, Rhetts and Ruckelshaus whose senior member, Gerard Reilly, was a former member of the NLRB. Brooks was allowed only half an hour for his argument. He began with a motion to reopen the record to show that Mount Hope, North Carolina, was not the alter ego of the Massachusetts corporation. In addition to the documents he had previously sought to offer, he offered the testimony of Butner employees "who have never considered that their employer was Massachusetts, Frank L. Daylor or J.K. Milliken, Sr." Brooks pointed out that the board's general counsel had used such evidence when it subpoenaed two Butner employees to Taunton for the hearing. Once more, his motion was denied.

The atmosphere of the brief hearing before the board was more formal and less hostile but no more favorable to the Mount Hope case than Whittemore had been. Brooks challenged the examiner's findings point by point, and offered the transcript of the hearing as evidence of "bias, partiality and prejudice on the part of the trial examiner to such an extent as to condemn his report as lacking in semblance of a fair, judicial determination." Brooks charged that once Whittemore had conceived the idea of a "runaway shop," "he has been at pains to conjure up a factual situation, bearing little or no resemblance to that disclosed by the record, which would conform to this preconception. This is the only plausible explanation for his persistent and blatant disregard of . . . uncontradicted facts disclosed by the witnesses and the documents in this case."

Brooks argued that the two Mount Hope corporations had been shown to be different, both as to ownership and customers served. He also denied that the company's refusal to bargain with the union before NLRB certification was an unfair labor practice and renewed his argument that economic reasons were the cause of the move south. He ended by charging that Whittemore had charged Mount Hope with violations that were not in the complaint— among them the allegation that the company's agreement with the union which ended the strike was made in "bad faith."

In his summary Brooks said that though the case was complex, its facts were not in substantial dispute. "The errors," he said, "are largely errors of interpretation and, in many cases, of distortion or disregard of, undisputed facts." He pointed out that most of the witnesses were Mount Hope officials, whose testimony was not challenged. "Consequently," Brooks said, "the largest area of controversy in the case arises from inferences or what the trial examiner is disposed to call 'inferences' . . . and his construction of novel or unintelligible legal theories."

The board issued its decision on July 30. It upheld Whittemore on all except one major point, ruling that though Mount Hope had expedited the layoffs of the final 65 workers because of their union activity, it had been justified in layoffs of the first 120 men. The board also ruled that the North Carolina corporation was to be held responsible for the violations charged to Mount Hope, Massachusetts.

There was now a race for the courthouse. Brooks, who had prepared an appeal in anticipation of such a ruling, won by docketing his appeal in Richmond, Virginia, home of the Fourth Circuit. It was a near thing, for the union lawyers appeared in court in Boston only three hours later.

In December, 1953, the NLRB asked the Court to enforce its order, and in January, 1954, the Fourth Circuit heard arguments in Charlotte, North Carolina.

The three-man court was one of the nation's most distinguished. Its chief judge was John J. Parker, who had recently returned from presiding over the Nuremburg Trials. The other justices were Morris A. Soper, of Baltimore, who was to write the opinion in this case; and Armistead M. Dobie, a former dean of the University of Virginia law school. Brooks realized from the first moments that the tide had turned in Mount Hope's favor, and he was confident that his case was won. If he proved to be correct, this augured a spectacular triumph for the company.

Attorneys for the union and the board, Jacob Minkin of New Bedford, Massachusetts, and Owsley Vose of Washington, came under sharp attack from the bench as the three justices spoke from their notes of the briefs. Much of the hearing, in fact, was spent by Minkin and Vose in trying to parry the court's assault upon Whittemore's findings, and the lawyers found themselves defend-

Portrait Gallery

Joseph and Jedidah Knowles.

Angeline Bourne. She and Frank Knowles were married in 1886.

Joseph Frank Knowles.

Carrie Dodds, wife of J.K. Milliken and mother of Robert D. Milliken, Helen Milliken Hughes, J.K. Milliken, Jr., and Ruth Milliken FitzGerald.

Joseph Knowles Milliken (J.K.).

Gertrude Cornish Milliken, second wife of J.K. Milliken, was headmistress of The House in the Pines School and a trustee and benefactor of Middlebury College.

Howard Wright Thomas, father of Mrs. Robert D. Milliken.

J.K. Milliken, Jr., J.K. Milliken and Robert D. Milliken.

Joseph Knowles Milliken, Jr. (Pete).

This 1975 portrait of Robert Dodds Milliken (Bob) was painted by George Augusta. (Photo by Walter Shackelford.)

Mr. and Mrs. Robert D. Milliken at their son's wedding reception.

Wedding Day. Mrs. John K. Milliken (left) and Joan Milliken.

John Knowles Milliken (Jake). (Photo by Fabian Bachrach.)

REGARD BIEN

Milliken

Family coat of arms.

ing the principle of federal interference with management's rights to shut down the plant in face of unfavorable economic conditions.

Judge Dobie commented that, "apart from any matter of unfair labor practices," he had "little sympathy" for the NLRB's attempt to run Mount Hope's business. Chief Judge Parker said he thought the board had been "grasping at straws" in its decision, and he joined Judge Soper in criticizing Whittemore's exclusion of economic data showing that the company's move southward was made to locate near fabric manufacturers who were major customers.

Minkin said he did not challenge an employer's right to go out of business in case he did not want to deal with a labor union—but insisted that the statute required all employers to bargain in good faith with certified bargaining agents of his employees. Minkin charged Mount Hope with "subterfuge" in an attempt to hide its identity and said the company could not legally refuse to bargain on the pretext of closing down and then establish a similar business in North Carolina with a new set of employees for the purpose of escaping the union. The judges did not appear to be convinced.

All the justices seemed to agree with Brooks that Mount Hope, North Carolina, despite its ties with Massachusetts, could not be condemned as a vehicle for evading the National Labor Relations Act. But though Brooks evidently persuaded the court that the corporate transfer was not proof of the company's unwillingness to bargain with the union, he was less successful in persuading it that the two companies were not intimately connected. The bench pointed out that corporate sleight of hand was involved in the transfer of machinery, trademarks, goodwill and sales organization from one company to the other.

But, on the whole, the judges were obviously sympathetic to Mount Hope. Judge Soper chided the NLRB counsel, "The board, it seems to me, has ignored this great national movement (to the south)."

Brooks pursued this line to the end of his argument, accusing the NLRB of deliberately ignoring the crucial economic factors that had compelled Mount Hope to move south, and he obviously won the favorable attention of the court as he described the long-term movement of the textile industry to the south.

"When Mount Hope was founded in 1901," Brooks said, "it was located in the world's greatest cotton spinning area. That area has gone south."

Brooks ended the hearing with confidence and assured the Millikens that they had won their case. Two months later, in March, 1954, the court issued its decision, vindicating his prediction. From its Richmond headquarters the court ordered the board's order set aside and denied its enforcement. Judge Soper's opinion held that the board and the union had presented insufficient evidence to find Mount Hope guilty of having moved to evade negotiations with the union.

Soper pointed out in his review that the previously prosperous Mount Hope, Massachusetts, had suffered a 50 percent decline in business by January, 1951, had reduced its work week in April, and decided about July 23 to lay off 120 employees. The court had clearly agreed with company testimony that the layoffs had come before union activity had become known. Soper also reviewed the travels of the Millikens and Daylor to North Carolina in the first half of 1951 when they sought locations for a second plant. He pointed out that Robert Milliken and Frank Daylor became owners of the new company and that other shareholders of the Massachusetts firm did not share the risks of the Butner enterprise.

All of the changes he described, Soper said, clearly portrayed "a business change based on sound economic grounds which had affected many other textile concerns." Soper also found that "there was no discrimination against union members in selecting the workers to be laid off and there was no attempt . . . to interfere with the formation of the union."

After a review of the board's decision, Soper continued, "After an examination of the evidence which we have set out in much detail we cannot conscientiously find reasonable support for the decision of the Board. . . . The glaring and undeniable fact which dominates all others in the record is that long before the union made its appearance the business was deteriorating and operating at a loss and that the managers of the enterprise were seeking a suitable location in the south . . . not merely looking for relief from temporary difficulties but from permanent adverse conditions which many other textile businesses had solved by giving up their plants in New England."

The coming of the union, Soper said, merely accentuated the company's problems, "and it was obvious to the company that if it could not make a go of the business prior to 1951, before the union was formed, it would be no better able to succeed after the pressure of the union was added to its existing difficulties."

Soper concluded that the union, and the board as well, must have been aware throughout that "the company, having committed no unfair labor practice, had the undoubted right to decide unilaterally and without consultation with the union to close its plant for economic reasons and to endeavor to save some of its investment." Soper declared that the board had failed to take economic conditions into account and had thus failed to arrive at his own conclusion that "the Union was not the cause that closed the business in Massachusetts."

Soper then declared that the decision of the NLRB was reversed and denied the government enforcement of the order. The union attorney Jacob Minkin said he was "speechless" and talked of an appeal. *Business Week* noted that "a lot of other New England mills that have relocated in the South are breathing easier."

From the day of its appearance, the Mount Hope "runaway" decision became a landmark in the field, a decision which was to be cited repeatedly by circuit courts and the Supreme Court over the next thirty years and studied widely in law schools.

The union's threat of appeal came to naught. After reviewing the case, board lawyers found that the District Court had established no

new principles of law in its decision, and, of perhaps equal importance, the NLRB now had a Republican majority, and its views had
undergone a decided revision.

Mount Hope's long ordeal was over, and the two-year-old plant at
Butner could face the future with confidence, free of the specter of
imminent disaster which had hovered over the company for so
long. But there was yet no cause for celebration. Other threats lay
ahead for Bob Milliken and his band of displaced Yankees in North
Carolina.

'Nothing but hootowls and rattlesnakes"

Mount Hope's North Carolina venture began in mid-October, 1951, with the arrival of a few carloads of veteran employees from Massachusetts at Butner's old army camp. The newcomers looked about with dismay at the aging barracks in the pinewoods known as Piedmont Village, where they were to live, and at the cluster of old wooden shops where the plant was to take shape—a row of buildings open to the weather, with large window areas swept by gusts of cold air. Not even the most optimistic of the incoming crews could envision the highly efficient modern finishing plant that would eventually rise at Butner, a smaller version of the mother plant at North Dighton. But Bob Milliken had chosen his cadre from the north with care on the basis of experience and ability and enthusiasm for the new project.

One of these was John Latimer, who had won his degree in architecture from M.I.T. only four months earlier. He was to direct the building and remodeling of the plant as his first job. Milliken gave him a free hand, raised no questions as to the cost of labor, materials or equipment, but told Latimer he hoped to run his first material by January 1, 1952. It seemed an impossible goal: "There was no power, no boilers, no sewer connections, no means of disposing of industrial waste. But Bob had a great gift for recognizing ability in others, and so far as I saw, he let his people do their jobs without interference. He had good people there. Not merely experienced and skilled, but loyal. I'm still amazed, all these years later, by the devotion to Mount Hope and Bob Milliken by those people who came down from New England to Butner."

In the first wave of thirty employees were several key specialists, electricians, machinists and millwrights familiar with all phases of metal and wood work. There were also supervisors with intimate knowledge of all finishing processes and problems. Only three men had been brought along to tend machines after the opening of the plant; other labor would be recruited locally and trained by these experts.

The weather was already bitterly cold, a forewarning of an unusually severe winter, and Mount Hope's pioneers were uncomfortable in the barracks, which were heated by small coal-burning stoves. Crews rose at half past four or five o'clock each morning, ate in the cafeteria of the nearby state mental hospital at six o'clock, then worked at the task of creating a new plant all day. John Brooks, the veteran English worker, remembered, "Time never mattered. I often worked voluntarily until midnight. Others did, too. We wanted to prove it could be done. My only ambition was to make a go of this plant."

But there were moments of nostalgia for New England when the

Mount Hope, North Carolina.

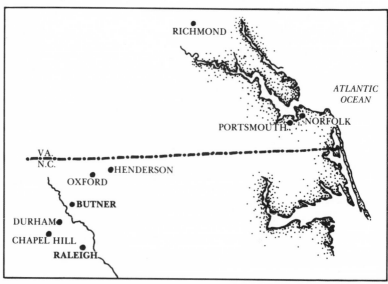

wind sang mournfully across the pine barrens of the remote, isolated site. Almost as one, the newcomers had rueful visions of the long-settled and highly developed southeastern Massachusetts that had been home to them. They missed the familiar small towns and harbors and the smell of the sea and the proximity of Boston and Providence and Cape Cod. Some Mount Hope people of the first wave (like the sixty-odd who were to come later) had second thoughts. Dan Dunne, who was to become night supervisor, said, "I thought Bob had made a mistake." Doris Booth, who had come to work in the billing department, said, "I thought I wouldn't stay. I postponed buying a North Carolina license for three months or more."

But the first of three hundred truckloads of machinery from North Dighton now began to arrive and the herculean task of fitting the new plant began. There were weeks of hard, demanding work before machinery could be installed. The crews began by installing power, steam and plumbing systems. A portable steam generator was rented as a temporary source of steam power. Once generators had been set up, electric power was taken from state installations and transformed. The process of creating a plant and installing machinery simultaneously was so hectic that the heavy generators were moved three times.

From the start it seemed that only Bob Milliken and his supervisors and their helpers believed that the plant could be put into operation in this way. Standard procedures called for completing the plant in a year to eighteen months, but Mount Hope could not wait that long. Milliken resorted to a bold approach. With the invaluable assistance of several Daniel Construction specialists, Bob entrusted his crew with the task. The life of the enterprise was now at stake. A few weeks earlier, Milliken had discovered that a New York syndicate, which held an option on the plant site, had exercised its right to purchase once the Mount Hope interest was known. Thus Bob was forced to rent and install machinery and equipment before he lost the cadre of skilled employees. He rented the buildings and bought a twenty-five acre tract adjoining the railroad spur as a site for a power plant; he was determined to buy the entire property as soon as it became practicable.

John Latimer was not to forget the building of the power plant: "I remember going out on Sunday, November 1, in a snowstorm, to put down the batter boards. We bought some used boilers and put them in place before the roof joists had been set, rushing to get the thing completed. We were actually using the boilers before the roof was on—and across the street, another crew was digging to get in the steam lines to the plant. It was like an army, building everything at once, while we were occupying the place."

During this period, while Bob spent about half his time in New York maintaining contacts with customers, Latimer pushed the project ahead. "I really never had to ask Bob anything: he expected me to do what I thought best. I went once to Illinois, to buy some used machinery that Red Staples needed for production. Bob left that transaction to me. Bob, like J.K. before him and Jake after him, had a fierce personal pride in his family and in Mount Hope. That had a lot to do with his success. Of course, the Milliken tradition was priceless. That had been set long before, by J.K., and the industry was familiar with it and that was a great asset."

The crews made steady progress during the next ten weeks of winter, led by a few men who became legendary in company annals: Eddie Boothroyd, the engineer, who had a talent for molding the diverse group into an efficient team; Sonny Seneschal, who drove the men to their best efforts in the tradition of master sergeants; machinists Joe Dube and Percy Charlwood, who knew their machinery as well as anyone in the industry. There were many other leaders, including Owen Synan, Joe O'Connell and Red Staples, the future plant manager and vice president.

Before the machinery went into line, men worked for weeks with jackhammers cutting trenches into the eighteen-inch concrete floors for the plant's effluents. Steam lines were brought in under difficult circumstances, but at last they were ready to provide heat for workers and for frames on which cloth was to be processed. Setting up the machinery was equally difficult, and more frustrating, for much of it was old—dating back as far as forty years—and in fragile condition. After it was torn down, this machinery had to be rebuilt by master mechanics capable of improvising and fabricating new parts. The work of Dube and Charlwood was crucial as they set up their lines with the aid of men they had trained in Massachusetts.

Bob had brought down about one-fifth of the machinery from North Dighton's plant since he intended to use only those designed for processing synthetic fabrics. He planned to finish no cottons in his new plant: "That market is fiercely competitive, and there are plenty of other plants in the South to do that. But there's no other finisher down here who's doing what I intend to do with synthetics." He was confident of success, despite the necessity of hiring and training a new work force. Mount Hope's traditional resourcefulness in solving difficult problems had been demonstrated in recent years, when the Massachusetts plant became the first to dye dacron successfully for the trade.

Milliken worked at a hectic pace to help breathe life into the new firm, dividing his time between the plant and New York, where he spent two weeks of each month maintaining close contact with customers and booking future orders. His wife, Jean, settled in a Durham apartment with their two young children and began a new life. She was tearful for weeks during the period of adjustment. She later recalled that Mrs. J.K. Milliken, Sr., who had come down with her husband, suffered as well: "Gertrude was in as much shock as I was. We all tried to stick together, but naturally we couldn't recapture the close feeling we had in North Dighton, where the whole thing was so close and intimate. Of course we would see some of the plant people occasionally, but we weren't thrown together as we had been in the north. There, we had simply lived together, and met on the streets, in stores or the hospital or post office. Butner wasn't like that at all."

But Jean Milliken, who was to contribute much to the success of the new venture, was a decided asset from the first. A long-time friend said, "She and Bob were exceptionally close and cooperative. Except for a short period, they lived quite close to the plant and Bob was at home for lunch each day unless he was out of town. Jean was a softening, stabilizing influence, the family diplomat. She kept up a strong friendship with Pete Milliken's wife, just as she kept up with the lives of the Butner families—weddings, births and deaths and all other important occasions. She was responsible for many of the traditional ties between the Millikens and their employees over the years. And on the outside, she had a wide circle of friends, particularly in Durham. Many people came to know her as a great lady."

Bob Milliken's assets also included a number of loyal employees who, like John Brooks, were determined to see the new plant succeed. "All the skeptics back home had predicted that Milliken wouldn't last long in North Carolina. They thought we'd soon be back home. We had to show them." Among those equally resolute was Clara Downey, whose husband had died a few months earlier, leaving her with a young son. Mrs. Downey had gone to work for the first time, in the remnant room in North Dighton, and had courageously come south to begin a new life, arriving with the first group at Butner. "I never thought of working anywhere else," she said.

The salesman Harry Corr was another who helped during the most difficult days of transition. He made regular trips to New England, seeking orders from old customers there and preparing for the plant's opening. The ebullient Corr never lost his confidence. "I felt that it would work because Bob thought it would work. He used good judgment in the people he chose to take down there, and because they were good people, we survived all the heartaches in setting up the plant. Those people were rugged workers; I can't tell you how hard they worked, setting up everything."

Doris Booth and several other women employees gradually overcame their homesickness and became mainstays of the office force. "At first," Miss Booth said, "I was always going back home weekends, driving all night to spend a few hours in North Dighton, then coming right back. But once the plant opened and we found our way around the area, things were much better. Life became good again."

The actual opening of the new plant to local job applicants was a big day for the Butner area. Long lines formed at the gates, an infallible sign of welcome. In this depressed time and place the pay scale of from $.90 to $1.18 per hour seemed generous. Few applicants had experience in the textile industry, but all of them had been accustomed to hard work since childhood. Most of them were farmers.

These people were to banish the prejudices of New Englanders who were apprehensive that their cherished regional work ethic would be challenged, perhaps fatally, by the parochial attitudes of the farm community surrounding Butner. The natives were to prove themselves willing and adaptable workers, the equals of those who had made possible Mount Hope's success in New England.

Though it was clear that Bob Milliken would not attempt to import the Mount Hope brand of paternalism from Massachusetts, there was from the start an easy, friendly relationship between management and employees that was to create a productive and efficient plant. The production problems of the first few weeks did not discourage Milliken or his supervisors.

Mary Cash, who was hired as an inspector, was representative of the new employees: "I was just a farm girl. I'd milked two cows every day before I went to school, and worked in the fields after I got home—we raised wheat and corn, cane, and hogs and cattle. We worked hard, I'll tell you. Everybody did in those days."

Daniel (Lefty) Jenkins, who left a construction job paying $.70 an hour to work in the grey room at $.92 an hour, remembered the coming of Mount Hope as a miracle. The black ex-baseball star who was to become a minister spoke with evangelical fervor: "People's eyes began to brighten up. I mean people on farms, lumber trucks, in sawmills and construction, stragglers on streets who were picking up bottles. Mount Hope made room for them, and some they didn't actually need. They paid more than we could make elsewhere. And that was a time when farmers on shares couldn't make enough for their Christmas money. The Millikens are a family that stretches out to help the poor. Mount Hope is not a plant of self-defense. It's a plant of many poor people, black and white, Indian and Vietnamese and many others."

In any case, Mount Hope brought hopes of an expanded labor market to Butner and paid wages somewhat higher than those prevailing. The plant was to be followed by half a dozen or more industrial operations which were to alter the local economy. The Mount Hope work force was about one hundred in 1952 and was to rise to about three hundred in 1980. The plant began as a non-union operation and sought to remain so.

Paul Harris and Dick Cash, both tobacco farmers, joined the firm in its early days because of the wages offered. They recalled primitive conditions during the first months. "We had no chain hoists then," Harris said. "We had to push all the rolls uphill from the grey room, and it wasn't easy. It was like working outdoors that winter. At least three-fourths of the first help hired came from tobacco farms. None of us had experience, but we found good workers among them, and the Millikens gave everybody six months to learn. At first we ran nylon marquisette for curtains, and that was easy—but then we got into taffeta and that was tough. We had mighty crude jiggs in those days; they had a leather belt over them, with a hook hanging down, and we broke lots of ninon."

Cash began in the dye house where there was a force of three, all superintendents from Massachusetts. "They were easy to get along with, but we did have trouble understanding each other for a while. I couldn't make out what they said, in those Yankee accents—and they couldn't understand one word I said. It took a few weeks for us to get used to each other."

From the start, there was little turnover at Mount Hope, North Carolina, and most of that was limited to the third shift. There was a persistent problem of seasonal absences, in the tobacco harvesting and deer-hunting seasons, but the company developed a tolerance for that and continued to employ men who left the plant during the late summer and fall periods. These employees included some of the more capable and dedicated, and foremen were glad to have them return. Larry Dean, who had come down from Dighton, found that older workers seemed to gravitate to his department, but he found them reliable, quick to learn, and apt to stay with their jobs: "I'd say the people around Butner compared very favorably with those we had in Massachusetts, except that an occasional one was illiterate."

At first, some girls who came to work in the putup room went barefoot, but they donned shoes good-naturedly upon request—though they were apt to revert to their old custom when it rained. The adaptability of such workers made possible steady improvement in quality of work, and thus in productivity and profitability. Well before the twenty-fifth anniversary of the North Carolina operation, Red Staples reported that the plant's production per man-hour was much higher than it had been in the Massachusetts operation. And, though seconds were plentiful in the first year or so, Bob Milliken experienced unusual success in sales to "downtown jobbers" in New York who bought seconds and remnants, and profits did not suffer significantly.

Local farmers were not the only new employees. Among the newcomers was Keith Thurman, of Missouri, who had been trained at Butner as an artilleryman during the war and had commanded the honor guard at the Tomb of the Unknown Soldier in Washington before moving back to North Carolina. Thurman returned to marry a girl he had met in Durham during the war. After brief service in a Durham mill, Thurman joined Mount Hope, where he began sewing seams. Thirty years later he remembered vividly the tolerance of Roy Stead, his supervisor, who "just took it easy with us and put the seams through without tearing up the cloth. In those days we started with 1000-yard rolls, never dreaming that we'd get up to 20,000-yard ones." Thurman took over the frame room after ten years on the job and was later put in charge of foam operations and all woven finishing processes.

Bryant Minor, whose family land had been taken for the army camp at Butner, returned from service to work for Mount Hope, putting rolls on the inspection machine at the minimum wage. After promotion to lot chaser, he was forced to leave for a serious operation at a time when business was slow, and layoffs reduced the work force. Though he expected to be laid off upon his return, Minor was given an office job and soon took over the invoicing department, eventually becoming traffic manager in charge of invoicing, shipping, receiving incoming chemicals, and the routing of shipments to some two hundred customers. "It's a trade you couldn't pick up in a school," he said. "You have to learn it day by day, as you go along. I was given every chance to learn."

Clara Downey was another whose career at Mount Hope continued despite a serious illness. "When I had major surgery, the Millikens took my son into their home and looked after him," she recalled. "And they insisted that I recuperate in their home during the summer, when they were in Massachusetts. They've been so helpful and understanding to me. They're very good people."

Sarah Parrott, who was to become purchasing agent for the firm, also found Mount Hope a source of unexpected opportunity. Fresh from a secretarial school in a nearby small town, she had never seen an electric typewriter when she was given a job in the Butner plant. "I filled wastebaskets with ruined sheets of paper," she remembered. "But with a day and a half of training I was put in the plant office to type bills of lading and reports." She made rapid progress and later worked in the separate offices where chemicals and supplies were purchased. "When purchasing was consolidated,

Mr. Milliken offered me the job of purchasing agent—it was un-heard of for a woman to hold the job. There was some male resentment, but it was expressed only once to me. The Millikens have no prejudice against women in business. I can tell you that."

By January 28, 1952, almost miraculously, the plant ran its first goods. The small crew had accomplished within three months most of the work that outside contractors would have required a year or more to perform. Though ruined goods were common for the first few weeks, and there was much to be done, the worst was over. Bob Milliken invited all hands to a festive supper of celebra-tion. John Moorhead, the Durham public relations man who now represented the new firm, was impressed by "the vibrant air" in Mount Hope's young plant. Much of this he attributed to the influence of the resolute Bob Milliken, who was, in this period, "an inspirational leader, rallying the men."

John Latimer, who left Mount Hope after a year and a half in North Carolina, agreed with this estimate: "It took lots of guts for Bob to come down to those old empty motor pool buildings, having left that great plant of a million and a quarter square feet. His great contribution to the project in those days, I'd say, was his spirit of optimism—his foresight. I think he was really the only one who believed that we could build a successful plant there in that place. And, of course, he didn't have to do that. The old Mount Hope plant in North Dighton was rented for a tremendous amount; all Bob had to do was sit there and live like a gentleman of leisure. But Bob would've been unhappy in that kind of life. He's a worker, and a doer."

J.K. Milliken, still vigorous at age seventy-seven, was also an important factor in the success of the new enterprise. Though he spent most of the time in North Dighton, he was a frequent visitor to Butner. The native workers liked J.K. on first acquaintance, as he made his way through the plant, speaking to eveyone in sight. "He never met a stranger," Paul Harris said. J.K. found the experience invigorating. "It's kept me alive," he said frequently. "I wouldn't be here today if Bob hadn't moved down here."

J.K. took the initiative in some company affairs in North Carolina. It was he who retained the Durham law firm of Fuller, Reade, Umstead and Fuller, which handled most of the firm's corporate matters within the state for a long period. J.K. also retained the Raleigh accountant Richard Urquhart who played a major role in the transfer of assets from Massachusetts to North Carolina and set up a new financial records system. The publicist John Moorhead never forgot J.K.'s direct methods: he began working with Mount Hope after finding one of Milliken's business cards in his office with the notation, "You are our public relations man. Be at my office three o'clock tomorrow." Until that moment Moorhead had known nothing of Mount Hope and the Millikens.

In August, only six months after its opening, the plant was running at the rate of one million yards per week, and progress was steady thereafter. Fortunately for Mount Hope, sales to old customers were steady from the start. Stuart Robertson of Robertson Factories had sent down the first order, for one million yards of curtain material. Another regular was Karl Robbins, whose success in North Carolina textile manufacturing owed so much to the influence of J.K. Milliken. Robbins had become a leader in North Carolina affairs, and was a prime mover in the development of the Research Triangle Park, whose future promised much for the state's progress. By 1980, over seventeen thousand people were employed in what had become the most successful research-oriented park in the nation.

Still, there were problems, and for some months there was not enough work to keep the plant running at a steady pace. Harry Corr was greeted on his return from northern trips by Spud O'Connell, "Hey, didja bring any money? I've got to meet the payroll."

There were also continuing difficulties in the plant. Steam power was still drawn from the faithful locomotive, months after the opening. Bob Milliken discovered that Butner's bountiful water supply was a mixed blessing since its high manganese content played havoc with dyeing processes and provoked serious complaints from customers. Milliken considered a suit against the state to cover his losses—until he found that North Carolina law forbade such suits. He then installed water softening equipment to treat the plant's intake of water.

Green local hands in the plant, in the process of training, continued to spoil cloth out of lack of experience. And by now many of the migrants from Massachusetts had returned home. As one old-timer put it, "After all, Mount Hope had been a Gibraltar of Southeastern Massachusetts. When they worked there, our people had jobs for life, in a comfortable, well-organized community that was geared toward the plant. When they were suddenly shifted down into the pine woods into a strange new world that seemed crude to them, without the fine schools, libraries, hospitals and other things they were accustomed to, well, lots of them couldn't take it, and they left." But Harry Corr remembered that losses were minimal. "Once they got out of those little concrete block buildings where they lived at first, and set up housekeeping in homes of their own, only a few families went back home. Most of the people stuck together like one big family. They brought in single people for meals to keep them from growing lonely."

For at least one night, however, the challenges of the first year in North Carolina were cast aside. The Founders Club instituted its annual dinner, October 23, 1952, at Hope Valley Country Club in Durham. Jean and Bob's fathers were there to join the festivities.

Bob Milliken and Red Staples combatted their own homesickness by having Massachusetts lobsters flown down on a regular schedule, and Bob played golf on weekends with men from the plant, Spud O'Connell, Dan Dunne, Bob Chadwick and others.

But though Bob was a more gregarious, social being than his father, he was sometimes unpredictable. After winning the tennis championships of his club on Cape Cod, he abruptly retired from the game. Years later, when he won low net in a golf tournament sponsored by the N.C. Textile Manufacturers' Association at Pinehurst, he also gave up golf. Milliken's bluff resourcefulness was displayed on the night he received his trophy at the group's banquet. While driving home with his wife and friends, still in evening clothes, Milliken was halted by a state trooper who came up behind the speeding car. Milliken hastily lighted a cigar and puffed vigorously to disguise alcoholic fumes, then politely accepted the trooper's citation and drove away with a sigh of relief.

A friend recalled another incident when several middle-aged couples were sailing off Cape Cod and came to a calm anchorage. When someone remarked that it was a great afternoon for skinny-dipping, Bob abruptly shucked off his clothes and dove overboard.

Though Bob had his father's intense interest in—even devotion to—the family business, he spent much more time with his family, in hunting and fishing, and in social life in general. He and Jean Milliken had been skiing together since the 1930's, in the days before chair lifts; they frequently attended football games at Duke and the University of North Carolina and enjoyed trips to Pinehurst and the Outer Banks.

Milliken was physically active in other ways. He had been a dedicated vegetable gardener since his marriage and insisted upon doing most of the work himself, from preparing the soil and planting to tending his plants to harvesting.

Politically, Bob was an outspoken conservative activist and a generous contributor to the Republican Party. In an era when such views were not popular, he wrote vigorous letters to newspapers, legislators and governors, supporting conservative causes. He also conducted private philanthropies in such secrecy that recipients, and even his wife, learned nothing about his role. On one occasion Jean Milliken learned only years later of his financial support of the local rescue squad.

Though his warm, outgoing personality and good nature made him a successful salesman, Milliken was reserved. A friend said of

Bob and Jean, "They are both vivacious, full of fun, with genuine fondness for people. They're sociable, but contained, and never 'pushy' or ostentatious. Despite their very active lives, socially and in business, their focus was always on their home and family."

During the difficult first years of the North Carolina venture, Bob Milliken not only provided the concept of the new plant and the capital, but his courage and foresight impressed all of those familiar with the Mount Hope project. One observer said, "He was both the general and the sergeant of the expedition, and his attention to detail was phenomenal." Still, as his wife remarked, "He had problems, plenty of them, but he never brought them home. He always left them at the office, no matter what."

Though the North Carolina plant was much smaller in scale than its Massachusetts parent, and was to remain so, Bob Milliken adapted many of his father's time-tested principles to the new operation. Within a few months after the plant's opening he bought a seventy-acre tract in the neighborhood and created a small residential area for a number of employees. He and Jean also built a home for themselves on a pine-covered hillside, overlooking a street where several of Mount Hope's key employees lived. Natives were quick to dub the area "Yankee Village."

Jean Milliken, who was happy to move from their Durham apartment, was somewhat apprehensive about living in the isolated woodland, and the prospect was not improved by Lefty Jenkins. At news of the move, Jenkins shook his head and said somberly, "Mrs. Milliken, there ain't nothing out here but hootowls and rattlesnakes."

Jenkins soon made himself indispensable to the Milliken family. He became the gardener and handyman, babysitter, taskmaster and coach to the children. Lefty devised both work and games for Joan and Jake, and once Jake learned of his career in baseball, Jenkins was obliged to teach the youngster to pitch and to play ball with him endlessly.

Lefty remembered those years fondly: "I took 'em all over Butner, with their horse and pony. I had games for 'em every day. When they got home from school I made them race, with the dogs, to the leaf pile—and Jake would always take off before I could count to three. We made things together for Thanksgiving and Halloween and Christmas. I taught 'em to make hats from paper sacks. Mostly I kept 'em at work, helping rake leaves or take care of the garden. One time some kids came up the hill from the neighborhood and Jake ran 'em off. He said, 'You can't come up here, unless you work.'

"He got to be a good little pitcher, too. None of the kids around there could hit him. And those children came up right. They were so obedient. Their parents raised 'em up to do like they ought. They had good discipline, but they came up friendly, too. And they're all business, like the rest of the Millikens. They know about work. They're all like ants, always busy about something. Even when Jake finished school, he wasn't given years to fool around. He just went to work."

Jenkins saw little of the young Millikens after they left home for college, but "they always looked me up at Christmas, and saw that I was all right, and came to my house, or had me come to theirs for gifts. And Mr. and Mrs. Milliken, they never could help me enough. They drove me all around the whole place, trying to help me find a house I could buy. They helped me, too, to get a loan. Through their help, I've got a house at Henderson and when it was paid for I got one at Butner—paid off that 33-year loan, too, and did it in two years. They've given me a teaching like parents. I learned from them, even when they were teaching Joanie and Jake. The Milliken men, Mr. J.K. and Mr. Bob and Jake, too, they all have just a few words, but they're so full of meaning you can go a long way on them.

"It takes remarkable people, in their position, to be so much help to a poor old fellow like me. But they've always treated everybody the same, no matter who they were. They always speak such a pleasant good morning. To this day, I often put myself in their way, just to hear them say their good mornings. They won't turn me loose, either, until they find out if things are all right with me."

As the company began to gather momentum, it became increasingly clear that a few key employees were vital ingredients in Mount Hope's success: plant manager George (Red) Staples; sales chief Bob Stegeman; technical director Felix Buba; and finance officer Mary Peed. In keeping with the firm's traditions, all had risen through the ranks, acquiring thorough knowledge of operations; their talents were well suited to Mount Hope's lean system, which provided no place for non-essential administrators.

Staples was a son of a former finishing superintendent in North Dighton, Bill Staples, who had developed a casein formaldehyde finish and worked with Doug Robertson to perfect "puffy dots" on marquisettes. Young Red had attended Bridgewater (Massachusetts) Teachers College and Durfee Textile School, worked in another finishing plant for two years, but had spent most of his early working career at Mount Hope until entering the Air Corps in World War II. He began at the age of sixteen, putting on rolls in the inspection room and graduating to the grey's thirteen-hour night shift before entering the Air Corps. He worked briefly at a desk, then as electrician, and was promoted to foreman in the plant's troubled "wet end," where a new bleaching range had been a major problem for two years. Within six weeks the resourceful Staples had the unit running smoothly.

Red had been in the first contingent arriving in North Carolina and played an important role in setting up the new plant. He was more aggressive than his capable father, who had stood in awe of J.K. Milliken, despite his tough, physical manner of enforcing plant discipline. As machinery improved at Butner, volume increased and more demanding processes were used, the contributions of the driving, uncompromising younger Staples became apparent. His intimate knowledge of processes and machinery, his boundless energy and extraordinary judgment won him a reputation as one of the industry's most able plant managers. He was soon to become executive vice president and director as well.

Though he was to employ other plant managers on occasion, Bob Milliken recognized in Staples a rare combination of technical expertise and a personable manner that enabled him to communicate effectively with important customers, suppliers or competitors. One foreman who worked under Staples for many years said, "People respond to Red, and do their best for him. He rants and raves, but he soon calms down, and you can talk to him—anyone can. He gets the job done. It wouldn't be easy to replace him."

Staples was almost as intensely devoted to Mount Hope and its traditions as were the Millikens themselves. During Jake Milliken's boyhood, Staples was resolved that the boy should grow up to head the company—despite Jean Milliken's insistence that they should wait until Jake had reached maturity and could decide for himself. "I always thought to hell with that," Staples recalled. "I used to see a lot of him when he was young—took him and Joanie to the movies often—and I used to preach Mount Hope to him, that the only thing he could do was grow up and become president like his father and grandfather."

The sales effort, an equally vital ingredient in Mount Hope's success, was directed and stimulated throughout by Bob Milliken. Though he spent about half of his time in the New York office, Milliken was fully aware that he must have strong direction in New York on a daily, year-round basis. He found that in Bob Stegeman, who had succeeded Al Curt as head of the sales office. Stegeman in maturity displayed all the ability Curt had detected in him as a youth. Though assisted by only one or two salesmen, rather than the force of thirteen Mount Hope had used in its heyday in Massachusetts, Stegeman covered the trade with enviable efficiency and contributed to the firm's reputation for work of high quality. By the time he moved into the position as head of sales, Stegeman was widely known in the industry in New York and soon became one of the most respected sales executives in the finishing trade. His insistence upon close, candid relationships with customers was a vital ingredient in the smooth, swift, efficient operation of Mount Hope's system. He took such relationships as a matter of course. "We're so close to our customers that we tell them frankly what's wrong with their goods, if anything. We tell them how to correct problems in advance, and most of them appreciate that. Those who fail to do so aren't really missed. If we don't have a customer who insists upon the highest quality, we don't want to work with them. Quality is everything in our process, from start to finish. We hear a lot about that from the trade. One customer told us recently that though he'd been in business only a year, he had made an outstanding success—and he attributed it all to the fact that Mount Hope had done most of his finishing."

Stegeman's close liaison with the North Carolina plant was important in developing new ideas for the trade, but he gave equal credit to his customers, from whom so many innovations came. "But it's not only customers," he said. "The chemical companies often come up with new things. And many of them—I think most of them—come to us first, because we're solidly entrenched in home furnishings, as the leader in the field of independents. They get our ideas, and then, if things look good to all of us, we go into the new project."

By 1980, Mount Hope's markets were expanding because of the company's reputation. "Lately, people have come to us from the Midwest, from Texas and California, and Chicago is a growing market. Most of these new accounts are contract people, but some are in the ready-made trade, selling bedspreads, curtains and draperies to department and chain stores."

Stegeman found his work a continuing challenge. "It's always exciting, never dull. We always have to be on our toes, because we work initially with a product over which we have no control—and generally the fabric has been made with no thought given to the finishing process and potential problems there. The major concerns of manufacturers are yarn size, width, fiber, and cost. And of course we can't send the fabrics back and say, 'Change this or that or that.' We have to work with it. We check all fabrics in the lab."

The sales director had no wish to return to Mount Hope's enormous size of past years. "If we had 1000 people, we wouldn't last today. We'd be too big and ungainly and couldn't control things. One reason for our success today is that the process, from start to finish, can be controlled by a few, a handful, of us, and everything can be kept pretty much in our minds. Oh, we have books and records, but on a day to day basis a few of us know pretty much what's being done, where it is, or should be, what has to be done to it. We can quickly pinpoint problems. If something goes wrong, just a phone call between New York and Mount Hope can usually get the remedy underway."

Stegeman gave much credit for Mount Hope's prosperity in the 1970's and 1980's to the plant laboratory. Stegeman pointed out that some competitors had inferior labs, or none at all, shortcomings which limited their speed of response to customer demands. "We can take something right off the machines in our plant to the lab and get the good news, or bad news, right away. Others, with less efficient labs, must run fabrics all the way through before getting an analysis. It may be too late by then. You can ruin a lot of goods in that way, too, and run up large losses."

Felix Buba, director of the lab since succeeding George Auclair at Butner, had graduated from New Bedford's School of Textiles and the University of Massachusetts and served as a navy pilot in World War II. He had worked in North Dighton for a year before the move south and developed his system of quality control through chemistry so effectively that Bob Milliken had built a $100,000 lab at a time when capital for expansion was restricted. In the words of Red Staples, Buba was "one of the most meticulous in the industry," and his attention to detail made possible the firm's policy of offering a comprehensive free test for every lot of fabric passing through the plant.

Buba's expertise and the dedication of his small staff made possible tests for every shade on each lot of goods finished, as well as a complete report on tensile strength, shrinkage and wrinkle resistance. As Bob Milliken once said, "Our customers know with exactness what their cloth will do and not do. There's no guess work in stating, for example, that a particular cloth needs no ironing. The test report tells it like it is."

Buba, who became vice president as well as technical director, was responsible for developing the unusual liaison between the lab and the operating departments, with the result that the precise control of such vital factors as temperature, humidity, speed of processing and the like had become a way of life for workers who tended machines. That close working relationship gave Mount Hope flexibility and speed of reaction that resulted in market advantages.

Mary Peed, another North Carolinian who began with Mount Hope soon after the Butner opening, became an important factor in the firm's operations, she said, "because of the Millikens' willingness to give a chance to anyone who's willing to work." As a high school graduate of 1949 she had trouble finding a job but took a place as bookkeeper in a poultry plant, despite a lack of training, and learned by following the pattern set by the former bookkeeper. After a rather harrowing experience as the lone office employee, keeping books, billing and receiving for an under-capitalized company, she resigned. She applied at Mount Hope, seeking any job but that of bookkeeper, but ending by accepting that post and hoping for a less responsible job later. "I found that these were the nicest people to work for. There was no pressure, but I was gradually eased into other duties over the years. If there was something in the office to be done, I took an interest, not in an attempt to impress anyone—I simply needed more money, with a growing family."

Her opportunity came unexpectedly when Edward O'Connell, the incumbent secretary-treasurer, left the firm, and attorney Frank Fuller asked her to act in his capacity. "He just sent me signature cards for the bank, and I took over." Bob Milliken was on a trip to New York at the time, so Mary was on her own in the office, faced with the task of learning how to make out profit and loss statements while acting as bookkeeper. "I just picked up things from the auditors," she said.

Mrs. Peed was an apt pupil, and as the company grew and its affairs became more complex, she became adept in all phases of its financial operations. The company's auditor pronounced her the best bookkeeper he had ever seen who lacked formal training, a judgment seconded by the Millikens, who gave Mary increased responsibility year after year because "she wants to do things right."

As director and secretary-treasurer in the 1980's, she was "essentially in charge of finances," as Jake Milliken said. "Mary would be on any committee making decisions on strategic matters involving major capital expenditures, such as where to invest surplus funds and the like." She was one of the few women in the textile industry holding such a responsible post in active operations.

Jake Milliken, in fact, regarded Mrs. Peed as a brilliant executive and money manager who played a major role in Mount Hope's success. "She's clear, sensible, creative, and also compassionate. She enjoys helping others. Lots of our people have gone to her for help and advice, financial and otherwise. She's well known in our area as a mentor and counsellor. And she earned the respect of the financial community—bankers, investment bankers and underwriters."

John Latimer, who had played an important part in Mount Hope's move to Butner, resigned in 1953 to establish an industrial architectural practice of his own. He found Bob Milliken generous in farewell: "Bob gave me a station wagon, surveying instruments, and furniture, typewriters, file cabinets and the like to open my office. His price was only $1000 for all of that, and he told me I needn't pay until my practice made it convenient for me to do so."

Latimer's new firm was to become one of the largest in the southeast.

J.K. Milliken continued to visit North Carolina in these years when he was well into his eighties. He sometimes came by train, but more often he and Gertrude were driven down in their large car. Though he still visited the plant, he saw several friends in the state, including Thornton Brooks, with whom the Millikens had become acquainted during the trial. Brooks once took J.K. to the corporate headquarters of Burlington Industries in Greensboro, where the old man looked about the lobby and shook his head. "You can't make money in an office," he said. Mr. and Mrs. Brooks also visited the Millikens in North Dighton and toured New England with them to meet their friends and business associates.

Jean and Bob Milliken took their young children to visit their grandfather during these years. One morning J.K. was at breakfast with the two children, reading his morning newspaper, when Jake overturned the cream pitcher. Milliken sent the boy upstairs to his room, but Jake climbed the stairs until he was out of J.K.'s sight and sat on the landing. Joan waved to him occasionally as she toyed with her food. After a few moments of this J.K. said from behind his newspaper, "Joanie, if you wave to him once more, I'm going to send you upstairs, too."

J.K. Milliken died in 1961 at the age of eighty-seven. He was buried in Taunton's Pleasant Cemetery after a funeral service in the Unitarian Church, almost exactly sixty years from the day he and his uncle Frank Knowles had founded the family business, in an era that now seemed light-years away. His son Bob, who had made the hazardous transfer to the south, was now fifty-seven, and Jake, his grandson, was thirteen. Only time could tell whether the family succession at Mount Hope was nearing its end.

"The old esprit de corps"

Mount Hope's corporate structure had undergone major revisions during the struggle to establish the new plant in North Carolina. The move to the state had been made under the temporary name of The Creedmoor Corporation, but the Mount Hope name had been resumed in December, 1951. At that time the new firm was capitalized with five shares of stock, of $10 par value. Bob Milliken and Frank Daylor held two shares each, and Edward O'Connell held one share.

This arrangement, too, was temporary. Certificates were endorsed in blank and delivered to company attorneys pending a final settlement, since it was intended that Bob Milliken would control the venture as major stockholder.

Internal fiscal affairs were complicated by the intimate relationship between the Massachusetts and North Carolina corporations. The new venture had begun operations with capital borrowed from Massachusetts, to the amount of about $1,500,000. The North Carolina company also agreed to pay substantial sums for machinery and supplies brought down from North Dighton and, in addition, was expected to pay $100,000 for trademarks, processes and goodwill. These debts were carried on open account, and the notes involved were renewed from year to year.

More serious complexities arose from the stock purchases made by Bob Milliken and Frank Daylor in Mount Hope, Massachusetts, before the move south was made. Each man now held 37 percent of the North Dighton firm's stock. None of this had been paid for, and each was in debt to the Massachusetts company by $565,000. Their notes bore interest of 3 1/2 percent and were secured by the stock certificates themselves.

In April, 1954, after some ten years of harmonious working relationships with J.K. Milliken, Daylor engaged in a bitter controversy with the family that was to end in his departure. Daylor was understood to have deposited all of his certificates in the company's safety deposit box in a Taunton bank, but J.K. Milliken discovered that these certificates were missing, and the ensuing quarrel ended only after protracted litigation.

Daylor, who argued that his interest in the Massachusetts corporation was being diluted by extension of loans to the North Carolina firm, sued to prevent this extension or the merger of the companies. He obtained a temporary injunction to that effect. Mount Hope sued Daylor to recover the $565,000 value of his stock and to compel him to return one hundred missing shares of company stock. Daylor's suit and injunction were dismissed, and three years later the parties settled out of court. Mount Hope cancelled Daylor's indebtedness in exchange for his 154 shares of stock and paid him $10,000 in cash.

From that point on, Bob Milliken's control of Mount Hope was virtually absolute, though there were minor shareholders. More than twenty years later, in 1979, when John Latimer wished to sell his shares, Mount Hope bought in several smaller holdings. There were two holdouts who did not wish to sell, Stuart Robertson and his daughter, who held their few shares for sentimental reasons. Over a period of years Bob Milliken had gradually given his children stock in the firm, until, in the late 1970's, they assumed control—a method reminiscent of that used by Frank Knowles with J.K. Milliken three generations earlier, which J.K. described as "like a feedbag held ahead of a horse."

It was in 1954, when the crisis over Frank Daylor occurred, that Mount Hope first reached capacity production in North Carolina, with profits finally becoming a reality—in contrast to a loss of almost $300,000 in 1953.

In this period Bob Milliken took another step that was vital to the Mount Hope future. By shrewd maneuvering, he persuaded the

Mount Hope Finishing Company, Butner, North Carolina, 1969.

New York syndicate that owned the Butner property to sell at a reasonable figure and bought the plant in which he had been operating. Milliken accomplished this by two almost simultaneous moves. First, he filled in and improved the twenty-five-acre adjoining site he had bought earlier and had John Latimer draw plans for a new plant. He then purchased an old truck assembly plant in the nearby town of Henderson and equipped it with machines for finishing garment fabrics and draperies. The moves were successful. The New York landlords agreed to Milliken's price of about $250,000 for the Butner property. The Henderson plant at first relieved Butner's over-worked force, which was then on a seven-day week, and helped to improve profitability. The veteran Roy Stead, who had come down from Massachusetts, was transferred from his post as superintendent of finishing to become resident manager at Henderson. Keith Thurman took over Stead's job at Butner.

But problems soon became apparent. The Henderson plant produced about half the volume and revenue of the Butner plant but was not an economically feasible operation. Machinery was insufficient to equip both plants efficiently, and there was much costly travel and shipment between the plants. Red Staples spent two days a week in Henderson in his attempt to oversee total production.

The firm narrowly escaped a natural disaster in 1955, at about the time of the expansion. Hurricane Hazel's savage sweep through the North Carolina Piedmont grazed past the Butner plant. A woman employee recalled, "The old plant building sort of breathed in and out, as if it was about to explode. The men hurried us across the street to the office building, which was safer. We thought we'd never make it across; the men had to form a chain and pass us over, the wind was so strong." The plant lost only a few windows, though scores of large trees were uprooted in the neighborhood.

The Butner community, despite the lack of cohesion Mount Hope's "family" had experienced in North Dighton, continued to be a hospitable environment for Mount Hope. Whatever Bob Milliken's intention in creating a second village for his plant, however, the contrast between Butner and Dighton was striking. From a town in which the company had owned literally everything from houses to utilities, clubs and food routes, it had moved into a state-owned community in which it was responsible only for its plant. The employees who lived nearby shared the corporation's benefits of state ownership. Taxes were low, and the costs of community services, such as fire and law enforcement, were borne by the state. There were indications that the situation might not be permanent, but it had endured for thirty years.

Bob Milliken's interest in the welfare of the Butner community was comparable with his father's concern for Dighton. As an initial member of the Butner Planning Board, he was responsible for attracting other industries to the town, thus helping to create a larger, more stable job market, perhaps at the risk of increasing competition for local labor. Through his friendship with E.A. Clare, he attracted the Athol Corporation to Butner, and he also influenced one of his important customers, Croscill Curtain Company, to locate plants in Durham. Other industrial plants in the Butner area in 1981 were ZapatA, Northern Telecom, Mead Paper, and Johns-Manville.

Mount Hope made steady but modest progress over the next few years. In 1961, a recession year, the plant suffered a serious decline in volume, the most serious since the strike-ridden days in North Dighton a decade earlier. Bob Milliken closed the Henderson plant and sold the property two years later. Due largely to costs of the idle second plant, the company posted a loss for 1963 and only a nominal profit the following year.

But Mount Hope was now on the threshold of its greatest opportunities. Developments now in the offing were to provide a base for future prosperity on a scale Bob Milliken had long envisioned. The first of several technical advances in Mount Hope operations came in the field of woven goods.

In this period the textile market was deluged with a variety of popular new fabrics, new in fiber content and construction, chiefly lightweight goods for the garment trade. Finishing plants throughout the American trade found difficulty in dyeing and bleaching the new fabrics. Bob Stegeman recalled one of Mount Hope's trials: "One day Wald Fabian, a good customer, brought in a polyester/combed cotton blend and asked if we could run it. We tried. The plant turned out 10,000 yards and the sample was accepted. To this day, I can't imagine how we got by with it. The sample was hairy, wiry, a narrow piece of goods as open as a screen, and a terrible cream shade. But the next lot was all right, and we improved rapidly. Al Curt had said we'd never be able to run those goods, but Red Staples insisted that we could, and we went on to run many millions of yards of them."

Bob Milliken moved aggressively to equip his plant for efficient, rapid processing of the new fabrics. He took Felix Buba and Eddie

Boothroyd, his superintendent of maintenance, to Germany, where they inspected the expensive new Kusters machinery, which was capable of processing open width goods on continuous runs. The Kusters firm had developed a new system of bleaching in chambers which had not been attempted in the United States. Bob placed a large order for the machinery, and the plant's capabilities were significantly improved almost at once.

With the new machinery, one superintendent said, there were problems. "German technicians came over to show us how to bleach with their equipment, and how to dye polyesters by the thermasol system, all so new to us that it was like opening an entirely new department. But Red Staples saw that there was no way to keep up our production if we ran a single strand of cloth, as the Germans did it. They showed us how with single strands, but Red asked, 'Why can't we run two strands?' The Germans said it was impossible, that we'd never do it. But we did. Red kept adjusting here and there until he got it done. It took time, but it worked in the end."

Mount Hope learned more about the process in exchanges with other American textile plants and through daily experience. Paul Harris recalled: "We learned the hard way things the Germans hadn't told us—rust on the chambers, for example, which meant spots on the cloth. But we learned and within a few years we had mastered it to the point that we could run that line with two men, rather than the six we used at first."

This advance gave Mount Hope advantages over competitors who continued to use the older American method of using J-boxes rather than chambers, which caused numerous rope burns of cloth. Mount Hope was soon running double strands at speeds of ninety to one hundred yards per minute, which substantially improved profits and reduced time on the line. In the final stages of the bleaching process the German equipment provided Mount Hope with maximum efficiency by removing from 70 to 75 percent

George Staples (left), Mary Peed and Felix Buba. (Photo by Jay Anderson.)

of the moisture from the goods rather than the customary 50 percent.

The next major step forward for the plant was its entry into the processing of knit goods, a field it entered belatedly in the early 1970's. Once more the skill and experience of Red Staples, as leader of the combined effort, enabled the plant to achieve advantages over the competition. Within a short period, Mount Hope's crews were able to sew the knit material into folds, so that goods could be fed into the jets under heavy pressure. After four or five hours, the goods were heat set on A-frames and processed at a high speed, made possible by previous drying on cans. At the end of the

North Carolina Governor Luther H. Hodges (left) and Karl Robbins at the announcement of the formation of the North Carolina Research Triangle Photo by Shafter Buchanan. Courtesy of State of North Carolina.

process, operatives could bag, inspect, yard and ship directly from the frames.

Staples recalled those days of challenge with knit goods: "We were in the black on knit operations within three months after beginning. It was unheard-of. Nobody does that. We were able to do it for several reasons: It was all polyester, which was easier than other fabrics; we knew our business—we set up a knit dyehouse just as we had for woven goods; we had lots of help from our friends in the trade who had been in the work for three or four years. And, most of all, we just worked the hours it took to do the job."

Though technical problems had been mastered, Milliken's market timing left something to be desired in this case. Mount Hope entered the market at a time when the demand for knits had peaked. Mount Hope, as it developed, had no more than eighteen months before prices sagged, and it became obvious that double knits were not the answer to the industry's prayers. Three or four of Mount Hope's customers went bankrupt, and though the plant had grey goods on hand as collateral, prices dropped so swiftly that the ensuing debts were only partially covered, and Mount Hope sustained some heavy losses.

The company later found ways to reduce the risk in handling knits, whose popularity continued to be cyclical. Mount Hope's versatility enabled the plant to prosper during such market ups and downs by shifting volume to other types of goods.

Another facet of the costly entry into the knit processing business was that Mount Hope had abandoned its traditional pay-as-you-go policy and borrowed more than $1,000,000. No more than one-third of this had been repaid when overproduction and slack demand brought on a market collapse in knits, with the result that the company remained in debt for about four years.

The double knit development had other important implications for Mount Hope. When market excitement was near its peak, Bob Milliken made plans to take in a partner and set up a separate knit operation—a move that brought a crisis to the plant. Both Red Staples and Bob Stegeman resigned. Milliken outwardly retained his customary calm, but it was clear that he faced a serious problem with the loss of his operating genius and the sales chief who was now regarded as one of the ablest in the field. Milliken called a meeting and asked his superintendents and their men whether they could carry on in the plant. The response was enthusiastic and affirmative, but future prospects remained in doubt.

Felix Buba and Mary Peed went to the Milliken home soon after the news had come to Butner. "Mount Hope will go on," Buba said. "No man is indispensable. Somehow, we'll find a way."

Mrs. Milliken had planned a dinner for twenty-four guests that night, an occasion to raise money for the North Carolina Symphony. The dinner was cancelled, and Bob and his wife left immediately for New York to direct a revision of the sales division.

Milliken also called his son, Jake, who was still in college. When he explained the loss of the two key men, the youngster was equally as reassuring as Buba and the superintendents, insisting to his father that all would be well and that the company would survive. Bob may have taken little solace from this reaction, but it was this incident that determined Jake to enter the family business. Until that moment, he realized, he had not decided on a career. He had not been entirely certain that he wanted to become a textile executive. But when he sensed his father's plight and realized how vulnerable the enterprise might be, Jake saw that Mount Hope offered him the challenging career he sought.

The Staples-Stegeman crisis, as it happened, was solved without disastrous effects upon Mount Hope. Red had gone to another plant in South Carolina—but reappeared at Butner a week later and returned to his old job, so quickly that some of his men who had presented him with luggage as a farewell gift laughingly demanded a refund. But it was not a laughing matter to Bob Milliken. As John Moorhead recalled, "Bob depended on Red and was shaken by Red's leaving and was visually relieved by his return." Bob Stegeman was also to return, after an absence of about two years in another job.

꙳ In 1965, after fifteen years of steady, if unspectacular progress in North Carolina, Mount Hope pioneered in an important new market development that was to usher in a long era of prosperity for the Butner plant. To add to their expertise in woven goods and knits, Red Staples and his men produced foam-backed drapery materials that were barriers to both heat and light and were destined to take the marketplace by storm when an energy crisis struck the country. The backings of acrylic foam were to be developed

Felix Buba and lab technicians, 1980.

first at Mount Hope—at least in acceptable market form. The company's swift response to the technical challenges involved placed it in the forefront of the development, and foam processing soon became the firm's leading profit center.

Mount Hope, it might be said, backed into its triumph in this field that was to become of such interest to consumers. One day in 1965 Bob Stegeman was shown a sample of a foam-backed fabric in New York, a rather fluffy sample produced by fabric, and Red Staples was shown another by a foam producer, General Aniline and Film. Though another company had produced the first such backing, it was Mount Hope that was first in the market with an acceptable product. Whereas the earlier product was thick and fluffy and could be dry cleaned only with a Stoddart solvent, Mount Hope's was thinner, flatter, and better suited for the drapery trade. After six weeks of experimentation, Staples produced his foam-backed materials, an effort that was the opening of a remarkable era for the "Cinderella House" in Butner's pine woods.

Using old machinery that had been stored for several years, Staples and his men began running the difficult foam-backed materials. Within a few months the outmoded machines had been replaced, and the plant crew had built a foam table atop a clear latex table, a task that taxed its ingenuity. The heart of the system was a machine that whipped air into acrylic foam, providing just the proper consistency; close attention and technical ability of operators on the line were crucial to the maintenance of quality. Despite their best efforts, Mount Hope's experts at first produced unpromising samples, rigid and with an unattractive hand, reminiscent of oil cloth.

For several months only one tenter frame was in use, and production was so limited that only one customer could be supplied— Robertson Factories. Another early customer was Pickwick Draperies of the M. Lowenstein organization, whose veteran merchandise manager Sidney Elterman was to remember his early efforts to introduce the product. "I took samples on a trip to Chicago, and they were so stiff and rigid that I slipped them onto a radiator before showing them to customers—so they would become a little pliable. I don't know why people bought them, but we got it going, and Mount Hope soon improved the product. I remember that Sears was the first to buy, and then everyone got it."

The foam market for draperies expanded rapidly as housewives and occupants of high-rise office buildings and apartments saw their superiority to the conventional drapery materials of the day, most of which required linings to achieve opacity. Mount Hope soon became known as the leader in the field, but Burlington Industries also pressed a claim through national advertising. This claim was challenged by Bob Milliken, who pointed out in a letter that though Burlington had produced the first material, it had been Mount Hope which was first to the market with an acceptable product. The controversy ended on a friendly note.

Foam backing was not a simple process, despite the fact that machines used to produce foam are identical to those used in manufacturing frozen custard. These fabrics were required to meet unusually rigid standards—to withstand five launderings, meet high tensile-strength standards, and still please discriminating buyers as to appearance and feel. And, as Felix Buba explained, the best results could be obtained only through the most closely controlled conditions. Temperature was especially important. A critical moment arrived near the end of the run when the foam and fabric were bonded: "If we don't crush the foam at the proper moment in the process, we won't get the effects we need." The foam was crushed under five tons of pressure.

Mount Hope developed a three-pass technique, with white foam applied first, followed by a black, and then another white layer, giving opacity with an attractive appearance. The plant was able to run these materials more swiftly and efficiently than the foam manufacturers had estimated, thanks largely to the continual efforts of veteran supervisory employees, among them Keith Thurman, who experimented tirelessly with temperature, speed and fans. Once it had mastered the process Mount Hope became the largest independent producer of foam-backed drapery materials, capturing a significant segment of the American market.

By the 1970's the plant had overcome critical problems and had devoted three ranges to running foam materials. This became the base of the plant's home furnishings speciality, which was soon to account for some 75 percent of the company's output.

To extend the company's market in foam-backed fabrics, Mount Hope entered the drapery print market in 1975. Red Staples visited several leading Italian plants before the department was set up, studying the equipment and methods used by some of the world's most accomplished processors. On his advice, Mount Hope made a major investment in a twelve-color Reggiani rotary screen machine. It was arranged in-line with a Lanly drier and curing unit

Mount Hope, Butner.

for continuous production. A new color kitchen and offices were installed nearby.

Printing became the second most important profit center in the plant, almost at once. The firm's success in effecting crucial changes that diversified and increased efficiency had been demonstrated once more.

In order to meet exacting demands of stylists, Mount Hope brought in Jaro Krska from a South Carolina finishing firm. The Czech-born Krska became the first presiding genius of the print operation at Butner. His work with new designs and general skill meant much to the early success of the department. He acquired a reputation as one of the industry's most talented printers.

Mount Hope gave further proof of its versatility in the handling of a variety of drapery materials, including all the synthetic blends in the market. And by now the development of Mount Hope's

Washing range.

major departments had made it much more immune to market cycles; when knits declined in demand, Mount Hope could be busy in woven goods or foam, and vice versa.

These technical advances in the plant laid the basis for future growth and profitability. At the same time internal fiscal and quality controls were installed. As Mount Hope's reputation for consistent quality spread, volume grew, and as the ratio of seconds and overs was favorable, profits rose. A new cost system helped dramatically. Installed in 1966, this system quickly improved efficiency by enabling Staples to determine the feasibility of running virtually any type of material. By 1968, with a volume increase of 13 percent, the ratio of sales to seconds rose to a healthy eleven to one—and a year later, with a volume increase of 37 percent, the sales to seconds ratio soared to sixteen to one, a new high for the industry. "This means," Bob Milliken reported to directors and employees, "that we are not damaging goods, and this is the cause for some of our popularity in the trade."

As a background to these developments was the still lively tradition of careful attention to detail that had begun with Frank Knowles in the nineteenth century. Machine operators, foremen, superintendents and executives alike contributed to the achievement. Under contracts with customers, Mount Hope was permitted to deliver 5 percent of seconds at half the finishing charge and an additional five percent at no charge. Though this was general industry practice, and competing finishers routinely engaged in it, customers did not like the practice because seconds were sold at a loss to them. Mount Hope was able to deliver only firsts to its customers since damaged goods were so exceptionally small a percentage of each lot processed.

The physical plant was also being improved during these years. Through the 1960's and 1970's the old wooden buildings were joined together and converted to masonry. Goats no longer mowed the lawns between the army motor pool sheds. The process of renovation, however, was accomplished with economy through the use of all suitable old materials, such as the original trusses and roof timbers.

In the 1970's, under orders from the Environmental Protection Agency, Mount Hope built a 4,500,000-gallon water storage pond for treatment of effluent and normalization of discharge. The pond was equipped with four fifty hp aerators and provided a constant pH factor and outflow to the state's treatment plant, as well as giving the effluent a homogeneous color. This substantial investment permitted the plant to consume its peak load of more than 110,000 gallons per hour and still meet rigid EPA requirements.

The power plant had been improved by 1980 with a new Babcock and Wilcox boiler in operation and two standby boilers at hand. The new boiler was equipped with an economizer to control flue heat, effecting a saving of 8 percent in the fuel cost of this operation, a significant item in a plant that consumed 10,000 gallons of oil daily.

The versatile power plant enabled Mount Hope to outperform competitors in some respects. The new high-pressure boiler furnished 230 pounds of steam, enabling the plant's frames to operate at 350 degrees, a level that most plants used gas-fired frames to achieve. The plant could also convert to low-pressure steam in short order through use of its standby boilers. As Red Staples said, "Mount Hope could lose a boiler, a generator, or a compressor, and still keep the plant running with backup equipment."

Further technical efficiency was derived from an improved system of handling salt, which was used to swell natural fibers for dyeing. In earlier days, workmen were obliged to move salt bags laboriously by hand, a time-consuming method which was abandoned with development of a piping system, fed by a four thousand-gallon tank of salt in solution.

Kindred developments in finishing processes themselves reflected the intense effort within the plant to devise quicker, more efficient means of operation; some of these techniques were directly related to improved profit margins.

Such achievements were by no means entirely technical or mechanical in nature. As they had since the days of Frank Knowles and young J.K. Milliken, the company's leaders of the 1980's regarded employee morale as the secret of their success. As Felix Buba said, "The old *esprit de corps* is what makes Mount Hope remarkable. It's always been in the plant, and it's always come down from the top—from J.K. Milliken, Sr., from Bob Milliken, and now from Jake. It's simply a willingness to work together, to do whatever has to be done to work out our problems. Maybe we're not always smiling, especially when we're working on one of our tough ones, but our people have always fallen to and helped as best they could. You don't find that attitude everywhere."

Delivery end of finished frames.

workers in Mount Hope's early days in North Dighton had been
maintained at Butner and contributed to general morale. One day
Paul Harris, the superintendent of the range and preparation, was
in the plant when Bob Milliken came through, pausing frequently
to talk with men on the line in easy, casual conversation. A newly
arrived machine operator turned to Harris, "Who's that?" When
he was told, the newcomer stared in disbelief. "You mean the *owner*
does that?"

This attitude was especially appreciated by men and women who
had worked in other textile plants and were accustomed to frigid,
distant relationships—people who worked for years with little more
than glimpses of the executives who directed the firm. Bob's success in this surpassed that of his father, who had seriously underes-
timated his elder son's gifts. A variety of incidents reported by his

Boiler room.

employees suggested that Bob Milliken's reactions were almost unvaryingly warm, generous and sensible.

Milliken once came upon two workmen playing in the plant, squirting water hoses at each other. He said nothing at the moment, in the presence of other operators, but returned shortly afterward with a quiet comment that won him new admirers: "Fellows, I got caught at that same trick once, but I was just a boy, and you're men." A foreman who observed the gentle reprimand said, "It never occurred to Bob to blow 'em out. He did it just right. I wonder if there's another company president in the industry who'd have done it that way."

Milliken's treatment of a receptionist, Mary Cash, under quite different circumstances revealed the same understanding nature. Milliken had been in the habit of leaving copies of *Playboy* in the reception room of the plant as entertainment for visiting salesmen and customers. Mrs. Cash, a devoutly religious woman, removed the offending magazines to avoid her embarrassment at every unfolding of the nude photographs.

Milliken once remarked to Mary that his magazines were disappearing with baffling rapidity. Mary feigned innocence but was soon stricken by her conscience. "Here I am a Christian," she thought, "and I've misled Mr. Milliken and didn't tell him I was throwing those things away."

She confessed to Bob, "I've been taking those *Playboys* myself."

"Gosh, Mary, I didn't know you read 'em."

"Oh, no. I put them in the trash. They embarrass me so much, when the men are reading them."

"I'll never do it again," Milliken said.

Mary found an amaryllis plant on her desk the next morning. And though she served as receptionist for sixteen years during the latter stages of Bob Milliken's active career, she never saw another *Playboy* in the plant.

The late 1970's brought another change in Mount Hope's top management as young Jake Milliken entered the firm and prepared for a career as president and chief executive officer. He was the third Milliken to head the firm in some three quarters of a century of its history.

Jake joined Mount Hope in 1972, confident at last that he wanted to devote his career to carrying on the family business. But, like his father and his Uncle Pete before him, Jake had begun learning the finishing business in his early teens and quickly discovered that the trade had grown much more demanding and complex than the "glorified laundry" business of which his grandfather had joked. His first mentor was Charlie Kay, an English-born veteran who was to serve Mount Hope in New England and North Carolina for more than fifty years. Kay was an exacting task master and was aided by a memory so phenomenal that he could frequently cite the numbers on bales of fabrics processed a week or more earlier.

Kay undertook the training of Jake as if he were preparing his own son and as if the future of the enterprise rested upon the youngster's grasp of the processes taking place in the busy plant. The observant Lefty Jenkins recalled Kay's role as a tutor, "He was a hard-driving, prompt, meticulous man, always alert and intelligent. He believed in Mount Hope doing the very best work. The love of Mount Hope has came from 'way back, and Charlie Kay had it and helped teach it to Jake."

After spending about a year at the plant, Jake was sent to New York to win his spurs in sales. He was delighted with the transfer. "Above all else," he recalled much later, "I wanted to avoid the syndrome of being the boss's son, always under the microscope, with my every move noted throughout the plant. I welcomed the opportunity to be a little more on my own."

He had worked in New York earlier during a summer vacation, when he and a friend took jobs as cart pushers in the garment district, working from 5:00 A.M. until 5:00 P.M., spending their daily wages on entertainment each night. "It had no bearing on Mount Hope," he recalled, "but it was interesting, and I did get an idea about the garment business and how it works. It was quite a memorable experience."

Jake served five years in New York sales before returning to the plant at Butner, acquiring a reputation for dependability and close attention to business. Many customers became fond of him. Fred Houston, the head of a venerable New York law firm, Otterbourg, Steindler, & Houston & Rosen, specializing in the textile trade, watched the budding executive with care: "He did a good job here, and was well-liked. Very dedicated and mature, and his ideals were high. Dedicated to his family, business and duty. And yet he's no dull fellow. He has a great sense of humor. Not a playboy at all. A very serious-minded guy, but with humor, you understand."

Houston, who was to develop a close relationship with Jake, especially admired Jake's views of Bob Milliken. "I like his attitude toward his father. He can be critical of Bob, and yet he has a fine feeling for him, and loves him dearly." Houston's surmise was that

Jake and Bob Milliken disagreed over the timing of Jake's return to the Butner plant. "I thought perhaps his parents wanted him to come home and marry and settle down," Houston said. "But Jake wanted to be in New York where it was exciting. New York is where most of the industry's corporate headquarters and marketing offices are located."

Of these days, Jake recalled, "I think Dad wanted me to come home and take over about a year and a half before I thought I was ready for it." He also felt that the New York experience taught him more about the plant operations than was obvious. Though he concentrated on sales, he also began a close study of Mount Hope's financial affairs. "Like Frank Knowles and my grandfather, I found that I could learn a great deal from reading balance sheets and financial statements. I pored over every report that came up from the office, until I began to understand our picture. I knew something about cash flow and cost accounting, but until then, knew very little about Mount Hope's situation. By the time I returned to the plant, I knew a good deal more about our finances than I had when I left."

The transfer from New York to Butner was rather gradual, as Houston recalled it. "I got the impression that Bob really ordered him to come south and that Jake might have been on the verge of rebelling. At any rate, he spent about a year of half time in New York, half at the plant, then a year of perhaps three-quarters of his time in the plant. And the next year he became President.

"Jake did just the right thing to prepare for becoming a manager. He worked in the plant from the bottom up. Next, he took to sales, in order to learn the relationship between the plant and sales. He could see who the customers were and learn what they were looking for, and also hear their criticisms and learn a little humility about his plant operation. I'll say this: he's a quick learner. A very quick one. And he keeps up to date. I've never yet talked to him about new developments in dyeing, chemicals or machinery, without finding that he was ahead of me."

Jake acknowledged that his working relationship with Houston was both close and valuable. "I suppose," Jake said, "that we worked together in something of the same way my grandfather worked with Frank Knowles."

If strains developed between father and son during the years when power and control were passing, there were no outward signs, but they were forty-four years apart in age, and their methods naturally varied. Still, one family friend saw numerous similarities between father and son. "Like his parents, Jake led an active social life and enjoyed sports, especially golf. Jake's unusually affable and courteous as all the Millikens are, but he does share his father's inherent toughness needed in the business world, and that fierce pride in the family and its enterprise."

During the collaboration between Houston and Jake, as the New Yorker described it, Mount Hope changed its banking arrangements and tightened credit controls through the use of modern methods. Through all of this, the veteran lawyer remained favorably impressed with young Milliken: "I've taken care of lots of young men coming into family firms. Jake's my star pupil. He's attentive. He wants to learn. He's as critical of me as I can be of him. You can't tell him just any crazy thing, because he thinks. And, though he's conservative, he's also creative, and it takes that in his trade, because finishing is an art, much more so than textile manufacturing, and there's a lot of trial and error involved. The art arrives when you can reduce the trial and error. Jake has to watch his technicians and ask them to explain themselves quite often, and he has the temperament for it, and the good judgment to see that they're all keeping up to date, including himself. He's up here in New York at least once a month, keeping himself informed and up to date, watching every angle.

"I'm getting to be an old man now, and I've been in this most of my life. I love business, really love it. But I hate American management today. Jake and some other young men give me hope for the future. He's quiet. Doesn't talk about himself or his business,

" . . . and these men with courage and determination, did pledge themselves to the new adventure. At the end of that first year they paused from their labours; then with renewed spirit marched on under the banner of freedom to the still unknown future."

—GLENWOOD FRANKLIN

Centerfold of printed program for Founder's Club First Annual Dinner in North Carolina.

Founders' Club

JAMES A. ASHCROFT	JOSEPH DUBE
EDWIN BOOTHROYD	DANIEL DUNNE
MEDOS BOUCHER	HARRY JACOBS
CHARLES BROADBENT	CHARLES KAY
CHARLES BROOKS	JOHN LATIMER
JOHN BROOKS	JAMES F. McGOWAN
WILLIAM BROOKS	JOSEPH MEDERIOS
FELIX BUBA	ROBERT D. MILLIKEN
RUSSELL F. CHACE	JAMES MULHALLOND
RAYMOND CHADWICK	EDWARD O'CONNELL
PERCY CHARLWOOD	JOSEPH D. O'CONNELL
NELSON COLLINS	GEORGE STAPLES
LAWRENCE DEAN	ROY STEAD
CLARA E. DOWNEY	VERNON STEAD
	OWEN SYNAN

Invited Guests

BEN AIKEN	FRANK FULLER
CHARLES ALLEN	FRANCES LAWTON
THORNTON BROOKS	RUSSELL McCOY
ALBERT A. CURT	JOSEPH K. MILLIKEN, SR.
FRANK L. DAYLOR	JOHN MOORHEAD
HOWARD W. THOMAS	

but he's an example of how well an executive can do if he works, I mean really works. Anyone who can manage a business successfully in these swift-changing times and still make a profit is doing it right."

In 1979 Jake married Kate Barlow of Durham, the daughter of a Duke University professor of French. Like Jean Milliken before her, the younger Mrs. Milliken had some foreknowledge of the demanding role of a textile wife. Her mother's family settled in Easley, South Carolina, and became leading manufacturers of narrow fabrics. Fred Houston, like most friends, approved of the match. "Kate's going to be good for Jake," he said. Their first child, Laura Hathaway Milliken, was born March 6, 1981.

As the 1980's opened, Mount Hope's personnel policies carried on eighty-year-old traditions in many respects. Advancement was open to employees, who were given fresh opportunities when better jobs became available. Only rarely was it necessary to go "outside" to fill new key positions. Milliken found that in skills as well as in dedication and motivation, there were usually capable employees worthy of promotion.

An exception to this experience was Chuck Revels, a boy from a small town in eastern North Carolina, one of several graduates of the N.C. State University School of Textiles hired by Mount Hope. After service in the plant, Revels was transferred to New York, where he made a place for himself in sales and became a welcome addition to the marketing staff.

Turnover remained low, and in several cases when men did leave the plant, they soon returned, to be welcomed "home" without prejudice, reflecting the pragmatic attitude of management. A profit-sharing plan for employees who became fully vested over a ten-year period was funded by a professionally handled trust fund, and other benefits were liberal by industry standards of the day; these included a scholarship program for any children of employees, paying a modest amount annually toward college expenses. Milliken kept wages on a par with other textile plants, and one of his superintendents said, "If a man wants to work, he can make more at his job at Mount Hope than he can anywhere else I know in textiles."

Approximately 30 to 35 percent of the work force at Butner was black in 1980, and the company found that there was little or no racial tension. Productivity remained so high that it was regarded as the chief ingredient of success, as it had since the days of Frank Knowles. In the absence of racial problems or labor unrest, Jake Milliken viewed the 1951 move from Massachusetts to North Carolina as a stroke of corporate good fortune. He said, "We surely couldn't be running such a large plant in New England under today's conditions. The move south was inevitable, and in retrospect it was certainly made at the right time."

The directors of Mount Hope in 1981 were Bob Milliken, chairman; Jake Milliken, president; Red Staples, executive vice president and plant manager; Mary Peed, secretary-treasurer; Charles Burt of Falmouth, Massachusetts; the attorney Herbert Davis of Greensboro, North Carolina; and Joan T. Milliken of Boston. The executive committee was able to meet at short notice, and a full meeting could be called within a matter of days. As the lone outsider, Charles Burt had been important to the company's progress. An accomplished engineer and long-time owner of an electrical equipment firm, he had advised Bob Milliken on a variety of company affairs since the first days of the Butner operation.

Jake Milliken, like his predecessors, saw crucial benefits in the small, lean staff and directorate. "The important thing," he said, "is that we can move fast, in a business that demands speed of reaction. We have no room for excess layers of executive fat." This size and speed remained as obvious advantages in the marketing and production environment of the eighties.

As president, Milliken practiced delegation of authority from the beginning. He devoted much of his time to financial planning and general corporate affairs, advertising, employee relations, and in travel to meet customers. Most daily operations were in the hands of Staples, Peed and Buba, whose skills and experiences were available to cope with almost any emergency.

Milliken was keenly aware of his strategic responsibilities: "We must anticipate trends if we are to maintain our reputation. Meantime, we are selling quality, service and delivery. If the competition lets down on quality, the advantage is ours." He is fully aware that his competition had most of the same goals.

In recent years, as in the past, Mount Hope had proven adept at recognizing and capitalizing on new trends. In 1979, the year he took over as president, Jake Milliken said, "We are not finishing a single fabric today that we were finishing in 1952. If we see a new trend developing, we have to get into the market before it peaks, or we'll be too late." It was obvious that the great changes between 1950 and 1980 had been industry-wide—but the ability of Mount Hope to keep pace had been impressive.

That familiar challenge was not the only one on the horizon as the young executive looked toward Mount Hope's future to the end of the century and beyond. He foresaw expanding markets for wider goods and with his staff had begun discussions of the possibility of building a new plant that might involve a major capital investment. "It may not develop in my time as head of the firm," he said, "but it's surely coming. The market is moving toward wider goods." A fifty-acre property surrounding the plant provided ample room for expansion.

A more serious prospect was the growing instability of the American and world economies in the wake of the roaring inflation of the late seventies and early eighties. Inflation's inroads, in fact, provided Jake Milliken with his first tests, which were serious, despite the firm's continuing prosperity. "My biggest problem from day to day," he said, "is how to cope with the continual price increases of energy, chemicals, dyestuffs and foam compounds. The prices go up and stay up, and often we just cannot pass them on to our customers."

He was aware that all other industrial leaders faced the same dilemma since he was active in several national organizations whose members kept an intensive watch on economic conditions. He was also active in the American Textile Manufacturers' Institute, which embraced most of the U.S. textile industry. The National Association of Finishers of Textile Fabrics, which his grandfather helped found, was still well represented within the larger group.

Young Milliken had a keen appreciation for the traditions of Mount Hope as developed by his grandfather with the aid of Frank Knowles, and by his own father in turn. But despite his pride in the developments of the past eighty years, his thoughts were chiefly of the future. "I have two generations behind me to build on, but I realize it is going to be up to me now. Whatever the future holds, it will be quite different from the past. I see Mount Hope in a positive way, with many assets. We have loyal, highly motivated people, plenty of room for expansion, skills and equipment, and, of real importance, we are debt-free. I have great plans for our company and our people."

It was an outlook that J.K. Milliken and his Uncle Frank would have applauded, even from the distance of that January day in 1901 when the family enterprise was born.

BOOKS BY BURKE DAVIS

NOVELS
Whisper My Name
The Ragged Ones
Yorktown
The Summer Land

BIOGRAPHIES
They Called Him Stonewall
Gray Fox: R.E. Lee & The Civil War
Jeb Stuart, The Last Cavalier
Marine: A Life of Lt. Gen. Chesty Puller
The Billy Mitchell Affair
Old Hickory: A Life of Andrew Jackson
George Washington & The American Revolution
A Williamsburg Galaxy

HISTORIES
To Appomattox
Our Incredible Civil War
The Cowpens-Guilford Courthouse Campaign
The World of Currier & Ives (with Roy King)
Get Yamamoto
The Campaign that Won America: The Story of Yorktown
Sherman's March

(For Colonial Wmsburg: *The St. Galy Tiles of Wmsburg:*
The Gardens of Wmsburg: Legacy from Past).